MAURICE COLLINS

BIZARRE & OUTLANDISH GADGETS & DOOHICKEYS

USED IN EVERYDAY LIFE -1851 TO 1951

Other Schiffer Books on Related Subjects:

Dictionary of American Hand Tools: A Pictorial Synopsis,
978-0-7643-1592-3

Designed by Brenda McCallum

Cover design by Brenda McCallum

Type set in Futura/Adobe Jenson

Photography by Jon Ball of Solid Imagery

ISBN: 978-0-7643-5132-7

Printed in China

Published by Schiffer Publishing, Ltd.

4880 Lower Valley Road | Atglen, PA 19310

Phone: (610) 593-1777; Fax: (610) 593-2002

E-mail: Info@schifferbooks.com

Web: www.schifferbooks.com

For our complete selection of fine books on this and related subjects, please visit our website at www.schifferbooks.com. You may also write for a free catalog.

Schiffer Publishing's titles are available at special discounts for bulk purchases for sales promotions or premiums. Special editions, including personalized covers, corporate imprints, and excerpts, can be created in large quantities for special needs. For more information, contact the publisher.

We are always looking for people to write books on new and related subjects. If you have an idea for a book, please contact us at proposals@schifferbooks.com.

All royalties from this book go to:

Doreen Collins Learning Disability Trust – Charity No. 1080972

The aims of this trust are to support the development of networks of families that have a member who is learning or physically disabled. By families getting together, not only does it provide mutual support dealing with the pressures of disability on parents and siblings, but it allows families to share information on rights available and to share experiences for the good of all.

The book is dedicated
to all the families, advocates, care workers, and volunteers that work
in the field of Severe Learning Disability.

I would like to acknowledge and thank David Bland, who has assisted me in researching, editing, and contributing to the descriptions of the gadgets and contraptions in my collection, and to Jon Ball of Solid Imagery, who, over many years, photographed the collection as it has grown.

Those of my family and friends who have had to listen to my continuing narrative of antique fairs, dealers, and the continual phone calls from those offering the weirdest and most unusual artefacts, knowing that I am the only person foolish enough to buy, I thank for their forbearance.

But I have to mention specifically my son, Paul, who administers the charity and endeavours to control my wayward spending, and to my partner, Janet Benjamin, who continually encourages the building of my unique collection.

CONTENTS

CONTRAPTIONS, GADGETS, GIZMOS, & THINGAMAJIGS YESTERDAY, TODAY, & TOMORROW

2-person Vacuum Cleaner, 1903

I was hooked from the moment I dug up—from the depths of a Victorian rubbish dump—bottles with pointed bottoms and others with marbles trapped in the lip of the glass. What were they for? Who thought of that? Like every inquiring mind, as I found out more, I wanted to know more. I hope these pages will bring you pleasure and amusement, but also a greater knowledge of the extraordinary inventiveness of human beings.

This quest to find out more led not only to this outstanding collection, but to a deeper understanding of the social history of the past two hundred years. Again and again, I came across devices designed to make mankind's life—especially women's lives—just a little bit less arduous. Take for example the two mechanical vacuum cleaners shown here and on page (p. 194). In the evolution of the "hoover" they are the missing link; they fit perfectly into the changes in society at the time: the need for greater efficiency as working conditions and wages improved a little, and everyone's desire to have a little free time away from the daily grind and endless chores. Yet these two contraptions had only the briefest of times in the evolutionary sunlight. Before them came the broom, right back to early men and women wanting to clean up a cave, and, later, the carpet beater. Yet both these turn-of-the-century mechanical cleaners still depended on muscle power and sweat. Indeed, you might wonder if they were not quite as hard work as the methods they replaced. Then, as suddenly as they came, they went, eclipsed by the invention of the electric vacuum cleaner. They had not survived the relentless drive from muscle power to brain power.

Everywhere you look in this wonderful collection, you see the same push from brawn to brain. Nearly every gadget has its predecessors, and many have successors today. Don't be surprised how often you exclaim, "My word, the Victorians thought of that already!"

Of course, some inventions were doomed to failure and oblivion; they were the answers to problems that didn't really exist, or were more complex and less efficient than the methods they were intended to replace. There is nothing new in this, and many is the invention or idea today that isn't going to make it, so some of the objects are hilarious or ridiculous, yet even in some of these is the germ of an idea that later generations perfected.

Why did they do it? The same reason people think up new gadgets, gizmos, and apps today: they wanted to make a fortune and make a name for themselves. Yet that was not all. Even if they didn't fully realize it, most also wanted to make a difference and better people's lives, to reduce the drudgery and increase the fun. Sadly, as many trips to the patent office have proven and is still the case today, inventors become obsessed with their concept and often spend fortunes in the development stage, often to no avail. I still find it quite sad to think of the man—it was nearly always a man—who came up with the coffee drink cooler (p. 194); a metal object you placed in the liquid to cool it, when all you saved was blowing on your coffee!

Patents were expensive, and to this day it's virtually impossible to cover your idea worldwide without major financial outlay; yet, especially after the 1851 Great Exhibition in London, inventors went to town producing new ideas or adapting old products to be more efficient. Not only in science, as Isaac Newton noted, do men and women stand on the shoulders of others to see farther. Even the great Edison only produced one totally new idea, but he improved many others that were already on the market, thereby making his fortune. Today's designers may well find something buried in this collection that may be adapted to fulfil a need in our present times. We can all learn from the past.

Alongside the collection of gadgets lies an invaluable resource of ephemera and books supporting knowledge about the artefacts in the collection, leaflets and posters selling the products, sales leaflets, letter headings, and even business cards given to the collector to provide a broader picture of the circumstances in which inventors and manufacturing companies operated. Perhaps surprisingly, the "mail order catalogue" has been the most valuable source of information on many of the objects in the collection. Catalogues from the eighteenth to the early twentieth centuries have the most wonderful drawings depicting each item sold, together with an often verbose description so characteristic of its age. I have tried to give an overall picture of the social condition at the time, the sales techniques, and the context in which many of these devices should be seen.

The collection depicts the different technologies available at various points in time. I hope you will look with the same delight on each object as I did on first seeing it, and I hope you enjoy dipping in and out of the covers of this book and find some buried treasure of your own.

I hope especially that you get as much pleasure from this book as I have had building this collection over many years. Like me, you may stop and gaze in wonder at the ingeniousness of the inventor, as well as marvel at the constant desire for improvement.

By the way, the pointed bottles and the ones with the marbles in the top that started this collection were to stop the escape of gas from lemonade and sparkling water. Enjoy!

1912 Vacuum Cleaner

FROM THE GREAT EXHIBITION TO THE FESTIVAL OF BRITAIN, 1851–1951

The Great Exhibition in London in 1851 was not in fact the first of its type—the French had held an Industrial Exposition in 1844—but it was then the grandest and it had a clear political intent. Though it was called the Great Exhibition of the Works of Industry of All Nations, there was no doubt who was the dominant nation; Great Britain was determined to make clear its role as the industrial leader of the world. This dominance in manufacturing had spread from the huge cotton industry and the coalfields to Britain becoming the workshop of the world.

Britain was first to nearly every technology. Her trading wealth, the power of the Royal Navy, and her comparative political stability gave her a clear advantage in the drive to industrialisation. This dominance did not last many decades. By the 1870s, the expansion of farming and industry in America, the vast grain exports of Russia, and technical and chemical advances in Germany brought world trade back into balance. Still an important player, Britain was no longer the only kid on the block. But in 1851, Britain was the world's only superpower. Over six million people visited the Great Exhibition from its opening by Queen Victoria on May 1 until it closed on October 11, 1851. The very exhibition hall—the Crystal Palace—was a wonder of glass and iron. Inside there was everything from a full cotton spinning machine to extraordinarily beautiful water closets (see p. 41), themselves a novelty. Two characters epitomise the spirit of the age.

George Jenning's finely crafted water closets can be taken as the height of Victorian invention: useful, attractive, and well-made. Articles such as these convinced thousands of inventors that they, too, could transform people's lives and make money. Following the Great Exhibition there was an explosion of inventions, gadgets, and patents for every conceivable device; the inspired and the desperate both had a go. The skilled engineer and the mountebank were both at it. Their efforts of every sort, from the wonderfully eccentric, through the utilitarian, to the downright fraudulent are to be found in these pages.

Alongside Prince Albert—the other main organiser of the 1851 Exhibition—was a wonderfully engaging example of the inventor and "doer" of the times. Henry Cole had an extraordinarily varied career. He was an assistant keeper at the public records office, a designer of teapots, an assistant to Rowland Hill in the introduction of the Penny Post, a writer of children's books under the pseudonym Felix Summerly, and the producer of the world's first commercial Christmas card; and he organised the Great Exhibition.

One hundred years on and things were very different. Britain had endured two world wars. The nation needed a lift, so the Festival of Britain was held during the summer of 1951, on London's South Bank and around the country. There was no Crystal Palace, yet the festival gave pleasure to ten million visitors. But the great days of the lone inventor were nearly over and the days of the inspired gadget nearly done. It had been an extraordinary century.

TIME & MONEY

Why invent anything? To save time by mechanising a laborious, repetitive chore, and to make money for the inventor and manufacturer, as well as for the buyer by saving them money in the long run. Apart from the entirely frivolous or speculative, nearly all the gadgets in the collection had these two primary purposes.

In this section these reasons for invention are shown in some exquisitely crafted machines that are all about time and money. There is the wonderful appointments clock for the surgeon or the solicitor's office that keeps track of time and keeps the money rolling in, as appointments do not overrun. There are the coin changing machines—a necessity in the gentleman's club. There is the beautiful mechanism of the pawnbroker's receipt machine, where wealth and hard times meet.

Although the nineteenth century was the Steam Age, it was also increasingly the Clockwork Age, especially for small and intricate gadgets. Most of these machines rely on clockwork, gears, and levers to do the job before electric motors, relays, and electromagnets were available. The results are lovely pieces of miniature engineering.

The skills of the watchmaker are found in some of these items; they are put to use in the most interesting ways, so enjoy the craftsmanship of the early teasmade—along with a timely cuppa!

Wakey, wakey! Rise and shine!

Teasmaid

A Birmingham gunsmith named Frank Clarke took out the first patent on the teasmade in 1902. Marketing began in 1904, with a range of machines offering different capacities. They continued to be manufactured right through the Edwardian period, until new technology caught up with clockwork. But the teasmade solution to the early morning cup of tea has continued to this day. This is one of the most beautiful machines in the collection and a joy to watch in action.

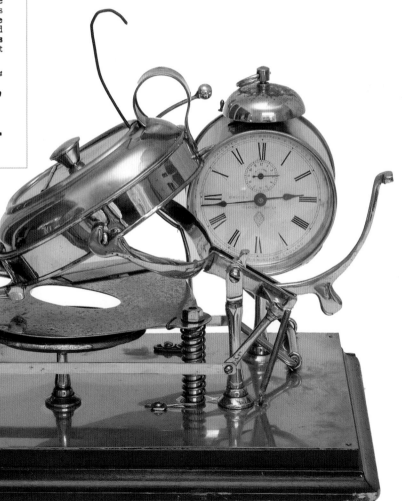

How Much Per Minute?!

Solicitors and doctors needed some way of timing their consultations to the minute. Then, as now, time is money, nowhere more so than in private surgery or the lawyer's rooms.

This cleverly designed timepiece was the answer. It hid its rather stern task in an elegant case. The name of each client was written on the bone tablet. These were placed into the top according to the length of consultation allowed. When time was up, the tablet sprung up and a bell pinged.

A quite delightful way of keeping to time.

It Was Only a Bird in a Gilded Cage

The Penny in the Slot Singing Bird

Have you ever tried to move a child on from a "win a toy" machine at a fair, in an amusement arcade, or at the motorway services? Well, here is a Victorian equivalent: less gaudy and more finely constructed, but with the same intention: to part you from your money. It is literally a "catch penny," but a very nice one. The bird sings a lovely song whilst moving about on its perch. A pleasant diversion for the Victorian family to enjoy in an arcade or at the seaside.

The Illuminated Clock

Look in your cupboard and you probably have a box of Price's candles, just in case of a power cut. Price is still going today. Well, here is an ingenious use for their candles around 1895: it's a combined night-light and illuminated clock. The modern bedroom clock is battery powered and does the same job, but this Victorian version is much more appealing and romantic.

Just in Time

Chess Timer

A charming Victorian timer. The players can see the seconds ticking away as the pendulum swings hypnotically whilst they ponder each move and the clocks themselves tip as the balance of play goes first one way and then the other.

Kitchen Timer

A simple timer in what was then the latest material—bakelite. No burnt cakes or overdone soufflés with this attractive device!

World Timer

This allows you to know the time in all the major capitals of the world once you know the time where you are when setting the device.

Chess Timer, 1930s

Cheque It Out

Portable Cheque Embosser/Protector

Today there is credit card fraud, but for as long as there has been money there have been cheats and rogues. These cheque protector machines allowed Victorian businesses to ensure that only the exact amount on the cheque would be paid. The numbers were stamped on the cheque in raised embossed print, thus denying the fraudster their opportunity.

Heavy Duty Cheque Protectors

Time Is Money

Savings Clock

This clock was given free to customers by insurance companies. Many people paid their household insurance or life insurance policies weekly. Only if you put the weekly stub into the slot would the clock work, so it was a great way to ensure the stub was still there at the end of the week when the collector called from door to door.

Projector Clock

Looking like a ship's chronometer, this lovely looking object was hinged, allowing it to project the time on to a wall or ceiling. Made by Eveready in the '20s, it was used at night when you needed to get the time. Just a press of the button and the hour was revealed on the ceiling of your bedroom. But what if you had turned over? Or did the instructions insist that you must always sleep on your back?

Timer

It is unclear if this Edwardian one minute timer is for the kitchen or the photographic studio when developing film—can any reader help?

Office Time Stamp

"No, Sir, your letter of the 23rd inst. arrived in the office at 4.31 p.m., precisely one minute after the latest time for replies that day." Presumably another stamp was used for the date, for this extraordinary device recorded the exact time on the document. Perhaps it could also be used by proprietors to ensure clerks were still busying away with documents right up to the final minute of their working day.

The Timing Stamp

Money Boxes, Calendars, and Purses

Calendar Coin 1899

Inspired! What a clever portable calendar for the whole of the year 1899. Next year you buy another coin. Can you see how it works? But why does it go up to day 37?

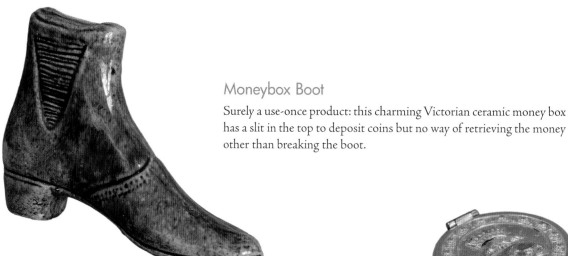

Moneybox Boot

Surely a use-once product: this charming Victorian ceramic money box has a slit in the top to deposit coins but no way of retrieving the money other than breaking the boot.

Sovereign Purse

Ah, those happy days of a gold coin equalling one pound, made in real gold and having real worth. This Victorian purse was specifically designed to hold sovereigns.

Time O Day

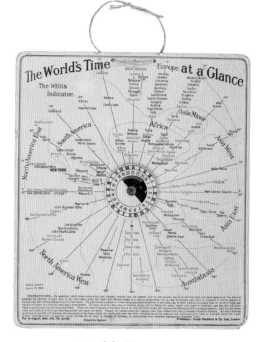

Worlds Time

And the Time in New York is . . .

What our smartphones do today with such ease—finding the time in cities and countries around the globe—could be achieved in the past with these simple but elegant cards. They were often produced as advertising giveaways by soap companies and the like. The map card is held by a central eyelet, allowing it to be rotated, then just follow the line to the place you want and presto, the time can be read. Very effective.

Bond Coupon Ripper

Bond Ripper

To enable the owner of a bond to easily remove a coupon for cash redemption this handy instrument, with its thumb and finger hold, allowed the owner to swiftly remove them. Particularly useful if the bond market was falling rapidly!

The Root of All Evil

Note Counter

No, not a mousetrap! You placed the wad of pound notes on the top, under the wires, then depressed the springs repeatedly, drawing each note off one at a time. Would a rubber thimble not be easier?

Miser's Purse

Looks as though it may actually have just come straight from Scrooge's inside pocket! Used by Victorian gentlemen to hold their loose change securely, they really were called a miser's purse, and, for the truly miserly, the bands could be tightened to hold the precious pennies even closer to the person!

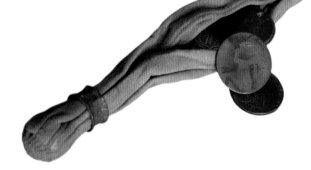

Coin Tester

Affixed to the counter of most Victorian shops, this little invention could test any counterfeit coins that might be passing from customer to vendor. Only checked the gauge, not the weight, but an effective deterrent.

Sovereign Purse

A handy little pocket coin dispenser for the Edwardian gentleman.

Mechanical "Alarm Clock"

A very simple alarm call that only rings once with a delightful delicate tinkle. Beautifully crafted and very well engineered, it works by placing the bell onto the dropping hook, then setting the number of hours on the dial. When the time is reached a peg moves the lever, releases the hook, and it tinkles—just once!

If that doesn't wake you, then sadly you miss the train or are late for work.

It cannot really have been a bedside alarm clock—it is too quiet—yet why would you have a timer you could set for up to twelve hours that could hardly be heard? Could it be a timer for consultations in a lawyer's office, or a timepiece to limit the length of board meetings?

If anyone has more information on this delightful artefact please contact me.

Just one tinkle!

Money Makes the World Go Around

The Victorian period was not so very different than our own. If you were poor life was especially hard, with the constant fear of the workhouse. If you were just getting by, the loss of a job, illness, or bad luck could see you fall quickly into penury. Even the rich could see fortunes disappear overnight. No wonder pawnbroking was big business back then; having and keeping money was a constant worry. Many the shopkeeper was diddled by a customer, and even the wealthy gent at his club had to bother with small change for the cab.

Sovereign and Half Sovereign Changer

The Sovereign Changer

By placing your gold coin into the machine, out would pop small change for the hackney carriage fare. The small slots would also be a good test of how drunk you were!

Cox's Shop Till

An age old problem! "I gave you half-a-crown."
"No, sir, it was only a florin." This innovation showed each coin in the window, in the order of transactions. Of course nowadays, "I gave you a twenty-pound note, mate!"
"No, it was only a tenner."—cue friction!

1st Talking Clock

This clock was invented in 1911, yet the first feature film originally presented as a talkie, *The Jazz Singer*, wasn't released until October 1927. A major hit, that film soundtrack was made with Vitaphone, the leading brand of sound-on-disc technology available. Sound-on-film, however, would soon become the standard for talking pictures, so in every way this clock was way ahead of its time.

Talking Clock

This fabulous beast was the very first attempt at having a clock you could not only see to tell the time, but also hear. The clock said the time every fifteen or thirty minutes via the cellulose phonograph band inside the cabinet.

QUACKERY

No age is without its charlatans. The get-rich-quick merchants are sadly only matched by the number of innocents, "the ones born every minute."

Yet, before we become too pleased with ourselves, who has not been taken in at some time in our lives? With the explosion of invention following the Great Exhibition in London in 1851, the rapid expansion and industrialisation of America in the latter half of the nineteenth century, and improved means of communication, it was inevitable quackery in all its forms would move from the dubious medicine man at the local fair to technology and the world of gadgets.

These pages contain examples of specious health claims, gadgets that did nothing at all, and devices that were more dangerous than useful. What would be sure to cure by magic could now be given scientific credibility.

Having a patent was seen by many as a measure of the efficacy of a device and not a mere bureaucratic stamp. Claims could be wrapped up in technical jargon—sound familiar?—to trap the unwary, and the unwary are always with us. It may even be there is a little bit of the unwary in every one of us. Let the buyer beware!

Eye, Eye, Beware of Quack Medicine!

Eyeball Tester

Tired eyes? Many an advert still starts that way. We trust today's products are more efficacious, not to mention safer, than this 1930s craze.

Eye Massagers

This may well have been one of the biggest cons known to man. By pressing the rubber balls, small projectiles leapt out onto your eyeballs, ostensibly improving your sight whilst at the same time a puff of air adds to the potential disaster awaiting the would-be patient. Beware not only false imitations, but the original invention itself!

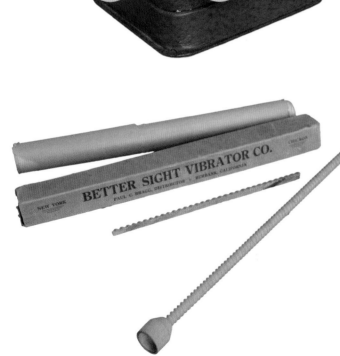

Vibrating Eye Therapy

Would you do this to your eye? Place the wooden cup against the eye, run the stick along the grooves in the wood, and, so it was claimed, your eyesight would improve miraculously. Perhaps best to read the small print, if you can.

The Ultimate in Nasal Quackery

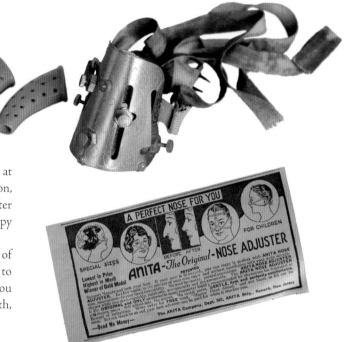

Nose Shaper

There is something sad about many of these bogus small ads. We laugh at the gullibility of those who might have sent off for this quack contraption, yet we can surely empathise a little with the desperate purchaser—after all, as it says in the advertisement, they, too, merely wished for some "Happy Days Ahead."

By adjusting the screws you can allegedly choose the desired shape of the nose. The purpose of the holed orange rubber cones is to allow you to breathe whilst you sleep with this monstrosity strapped to your face—you are meant to insert them into your nostrils. The whole thing is, in truth, sad and really rather gruesome.

A Shocking Massage

Over the years, electricity has been posited as the cure for all manner of ailments. Here are three patented devices with a shocking reputation.

Electric Chain Belt

This one doubles the effect—not only can you get your therapeutic shock when wearing it as a belt but you can also hold the handles and be totally cured!

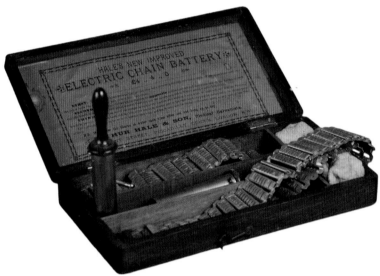

Electric Head Massager

Battery operated, this 1930s brush is supposed to stimulate hair growth, assuming you're not bald as a coot already, of course!

Electric Massager

This one really gives you a going over! The plastic fingers vibrate to pummel your body whilst the metal coils give you an electric shock. If you haven't had enough of the treatment, you can increase the voltage by moving the switch. Rather you than me!

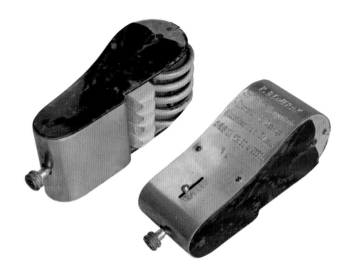

"The Wind," Sea, and Air

Wind Pills

Straight to the point—at least you can't say you don't know what it is meant to cure. This original box of Victorian pills was the indigestion medicine of the day, getting rid of "the wind!"

Seasick Plaster

A novel method of stopping seasickness: just place it on your chest and the queasiness is relieved. This "sticking plaster" admits it contains no medicine. From as late as the 1930s, it has the air of quackery—but did it work?

Vapour Maker

Doubling as a light and a method of turning pastilles into health-giving vapours for a range of ailments, this very common Edwardian contraption was found in many homes. We are not sure if it had any effect on one's health, but it possibly gave some relief, especially to those with bronchitis or chesty coughs.

Hair Restorer

BASTIAN BROS. & BASTIAN,
Clothiers,
629 Hamilton St., Allentown, Pa.

Hair Restorer

BASTIAN BROS. & BASTIAN,
Clothiers,
629 Hamilton St., Allentown, Pa.

Hair Restorer

BASTIAN BROS. & BASTIAN,
Clothiers,
629 Hamilton St., Allentown, Pa.

A Head of Hair

Hair Restorer

A postcard be sent as a sales reminder
to gentlemen customers.

Keep turning the heads on this delightful sales
card and the bald gent on the left ends up with a
luxuriant beard and a full head of hair, but only
by using the amazing "hair elixir." It's a rather clever
joke, though the advertiser is actually a clothier.

Tea, Gout, and Rheumatism

Quack Medicine

Pots of Holloway's ointments sold in the millions. It was one of the most popular
Victorian medicines. Different ointments claimed to cure different illnesses, in this
case gout and rheumatism. But were the ointments all the same apart from their colour?

Poor Man's Friend

Pity the poor man—even his last halfpenny was extracted
from him for this Victorian "Cure All" ointment.

Tea Strainer

What's so cute about this 1890s strainer is that it claims it is
non-poisonous—what must the competition have been like?

Asthma Curing Necklace

Sadly, this is a textbook case of quackery. Over the years, many unscrupulous individuals have preyed on the sick. Most of the quack medicines of the nineteenth century were cure-alls aimed at those with niggling complaints, tiredness, and lethargy. Of course, many of these "weak" individuals were probably suffering from genuine but undiagnosed illnesses. Nevertheless, many of these cure-alls were only a fine line away from pick-me-ups and tonics.

But here is a quack medicine giving unfounded hope to sufferers of a known and potentially life-threatening condition; this gives added poignancy to this device from the late Edwardian period.

It is in fact claimed to be made from amber, but is of course a plastic material that has been formed and coloured to look like the original natural substance.

The booklet accompanying this device has a range of illustrations. In the picture opposite you see the sufferer "in despair"; later in the booklet you see her with a smile and the words "much happier."

As usual in quack medication, they have a range of letters in the booklet from people that have used the cure, from royalty to famous politicians—all made up of course. Some of the claims are totally outrageous, but desperate people will always want to believe.

Shocking Cure-All!

Cure-All Electric Belts

This late-nineteenth century belt was an example of how the mystery of electricity generated its own industry. Seemingly no ailment could not be cured by the "magic" of electricity.

Just as many with poor health still reach out today for something new to provide relief, so the Victorians clutched at electricity and magnetism.

The batteries, held in small pockets, were apparently recharged with cider vinegar and water.

"The Quack Doctor
Will See You Now"

So long as there is pain, illness, and disease there will be those who prey on the vulnerable with the latest "cure all."

Wafer Paper

What a great idea—if only it worked. Many pills and medicines tasted foul, so wrap them in this wafer paper, swallow, and no bad taste. I'm not sure I swallow that, and I can't see the paper being easy to swallow, either!

Voltaic Discs

The discovery of electricity led many to believe it had magical healing powers. This is another example of those in pain being exploited and deceived by unscrupulous claims. The list of ailments these two metal discs was supposed to heal is astonishing, and don't forget it has "Never Been Known To Fail!"

Finger Straightener

A severe way of straightening fingers—cosmetic or prescribed?

Purifying Quackery

The Victorian period gave rise to thousands of charlatans practising the art of verbal and written persuasion to have citizens purchase the latest nostrum to solve genuine or perceived medical or emotional problems. The flyers they used—sent either by mail or distributed at public gatherings like fairs or circuses—played on the vulnerability of the sick, the fear of medical bills, and the dread of contagious diseases—in this case, even suggesting quack medicine could prevent something as serious as cholera.

Blood Purifier Flyer

The most interesting aspect of this particular leaflet is the depiction of the Victorian era housewife whose task above all else is to sweep the floor and housekeep. Many of these sales pitches for tonics and cure-alls were directed at women. Despite a hundred years of suffragettes and the women's movement, not a little of this same blatant stereotyping of women as weak, over-emotional, anaemic domestics can still be found in newspapers and on the Internet today

Just check out the expressions on the women's faces before and after taking the medicine.

Slimming Apparatus

This dates from the 1950s. It uses the names of two adagio dancers of the period—adagio dancers were performers of acrobatic dance, a sort of cross between ballet and modern-day aerobics.

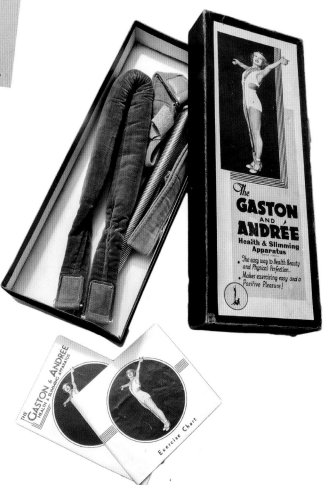

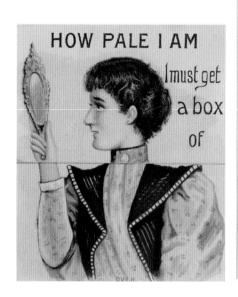

How Pale I Am!

Jolly Duchess Pills

Over the years, many products have targeted women's complexion and general health, yet over time conventions have changed, so that, while Jolly's "Duchess" pills were meant to bring rosiness to cheeks, just a few years before pale female faces were admired.

From the 1930s on there were more and more products for slimming, including mechanical slimming aids, such as the Gaston and Andrée apparatus.

Metamorphic Advertising Card

By turning up the bottom half of this card the rosy-cheeked woman appears, banishing her pale former self after having taken one of Mr. Jolly's pills.

Ultimate Quackery

Medicated Snuff

The medical claims of the curative effects of many spurious products sold during the Victorian period were generally outrageous, but this beats the lot! As you can see, it claims to "promote or effect a speedy recovery" after you have been drowned! But don't depend on it at the seaside, as it says this is only effective if it is first put into boiled vinegar before being administered—you would have to rush to the fish and chip shop!

Not content with this, they go on to list nearly every other known disease or condition, from gout to putrefaction, and assure the reader that magical medicated snuff will cure the lot. Perhaps, like Jerome K. Jerome in *Three Men in a Boat*, the only illness it can't cope with is Housemaid's Knee!

NEW FANGLED INNOVATIONS

A lot of the gadgets in the collection are small or mechanical inventions from the nineteenth century and the early years of the twentieth. They are the product of the second Industrial Revolution, as new chemicals were developed and manufacturers moved to meet the needs of the mass market. But the technological revolution was just over the horizon.

Here are some of the first signs of the miniature and electronic age to come. Some of the contraptions, such as the electrical dinner gong, were lost in the great social changes of the first half of the twentieth century, but others—the camera and the radio—changed society itself.

After the mechanical revolution came the revolution in communication, which is still going on at a dizzying pace today. Most of the items in this part of the collection were anything but gimcrack devices—they used the most advanced technologies of their day.

Perhaps most interesting is the combined portable radio camera from the thirties—the nearest thing in the collection to the smartphones of today.

The Cat's Whisker

Crystal Set with Earphones

This beautifully preserved example of a "crystal set" is a very early
example from between 1922 and 1924. For the first five years of radio,
all radio receivers—manufactured by firms like Marconi and Ericsson—
had to carry the BBC stamp; a useful source of revenue for what was
then the British Broadcasting Company.

Crystal sets relied only on the energy from radio waves to produce
sound so they needed no external power source. They worked
by passing a thin wire—the "cat's whisker"—over a mineral
crystal, allowing you to tune into radio broadcasts. Without
amplification they were very quiet, requiring earphones,
and so could only be listened to by an individual. Valve
radios were soon found to be superior, producing
amplified sound.

These sets came back into their own during WWII,
where their mobility and lack of a need of a power supply
made them ideal for soldiers in the field, where they were
nicknamed "foxhole receivers."

Sound Communication

World's Smallest Record

This tiny record from the 1920s claimed to be the world's smallest, having a
radius of just one inch, and yet was still playable on a normal gramophone
of the period. And the recording?—"God Save the King."

Electric Dinner Gong

Also from the 1920s, this battery-driven gong would, by pressing the
switch, call the entire household to dinner. But why is it electrical? Surely
it would be easier just to use a manual gong. Perhaps another example
of an over-elaborate use of a recent technology.

Has the Balloon Gone Up?

French Altimeter?

One of the delights of collecting is coming across an interesting item whose function is a mystery and at which one can, initially, only guess. Everyone likes to play the detective, so trying to find its real use only adds to the pleasure.

Here is a good example. It is clearly a barometer of some sort, yet its precise function is still a mystery. The consensus of opinion is that this is a pressure gauge used in gas balloons, acting as an altimeter: as the balloon rises, the height can be judged from the falling pressure.

Can any reader cast further light on the function of this example of fine French engineering?

A Typewriter Like No Other

After their invention in the 1860s, typewriters quickly became indispensable tools for practically all writing other than personal correspondence. They were widely used by professional writers, in offices, and for business correspondence in private homes.

Victoria Typewriter

The Victoria was a primitive index typewriter produced in Germany for the French market. In Germany, the machine was sold as the Famos. The operation of the machine was simple. The index held eighty-four characters in alphabetical order, including capitals, numbers, and punctuation marks. By turning the knob on the back of the circular index the letter was brought into position. Pressing the button on the side brought the index wheel down onto the paper. Two rollers inked the typeface. The peculiar bit was the paper was fixed around the cylindrical platen and the platen itself also had to be turned one space to print the next letter. To write the next line, the entire index had to be moved one step along the length of the platen. Extraordinarily fiddly and time-consuming, yet somehow rather elegant. The Victoria presented here came in a beautiful miniature office box with its own special stationery.

A very unusual writing machine.

Smart Technology Thirties Style

Radio Camera

Everything has its progenitor, and here is an early attempt from the 1930s to combine more than one technology in a portable device; not quite the smartphone of today, but a step in that direction. Here, the inventor has combined a battery-operated radio set with a camera. The idea, we assume, was to take this on a picnic, listening to big-band music before taking a family snap. Of course, just like today's intrusive mobile devices, maybe the other holidaymakers would have been cursing that flashy family with their abominable outdoor wireless!

Fares Please

Ticket Dispensers

Note to younger readers: believe it or not, just a few years ago every bus had a conductor on board collecting your fare money and giving you a ticket to your destination. Female conductors were called "clippies."

These ticket machines were slung round the conductor's neck on one side with a big leather money bag for change on the other.

Here are two ticket machines from the 1950s. These machines printed the value and other details on the ticket and kept a record of tickets issued so the fares and the money collected could be tallied at the end of the day.

Before these machines, clippies had stacks of tickets of every value in a slung holder. As they issued them, they clipped the ticket—hence the name.

Can You Hear Me?

Intercom

There is something especially appealing about electrical gadgets set into wooden frames; they suggest a time of solidity and continuity, and yet many would be out of date within a few years, just as today. This example from the 1920s could be used in an office or a stately home.

Servants' Whistle

Everyone knew who was boss with the intercom, but at least it was a two-way conversation. This earlier device seems to spell out the relationship a little too clearly; it would be kept in the drawing room to summon the butler. Of course, if the butler did not come running, perhaps the dog would!

Adding Up to a Computer

Mechanical Organiser Memory

This was being manufactured in France in 1925, and is considered one of the first computing machines, if not an actual computer. It is driven by clockwork, has a clock and an alarm and, most importantly, the ability to work out times of meetings and alert you to those times. Long before the electronic personal organiser or Outlook®, here was a device for the high-flying manager. The pad in the middle is more prosaic—a simple pen and paper aide memoir.

Number Counter

From counting sheep to ticking off the number of people through a turnstile, this early mechanical counter clicked away with the dab of a hand.

Line Counter

A similar device attached to a typewriter. It does need the typist to depress the lever every time a line is completed so it is a bit of a chore, but it gets the job done, and long before word processors. Now, how long had that essay to be?

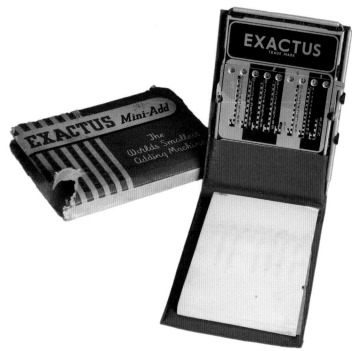

Being Very Calculating

Calculator Operated by a Stylus

A simple adding machine. To add up you just pulled down the numbers being totalled with a stylus and the answer appeared in the window at the top of the machine. For those not familiar with the abacus.

Pen and Pencil Case Calculator

This natty school item from around the 1930s had the dual purpose of being a multiplication calculator on the outside and a pencil case on the inside. It contained a pen, pencil, and ruler, and had a five inch measure on the casing. Just the job if you had never really mastered your tables!

Subtraction Calculator

Presumably aimed at shopkeepers to work out the change they should give, another machine that uses a stylus to get results. In this case it only subtracts. But what if the customer has bought three items and you are struggling to add them up, never mind give the correct change for the ten shilling note being brandished?

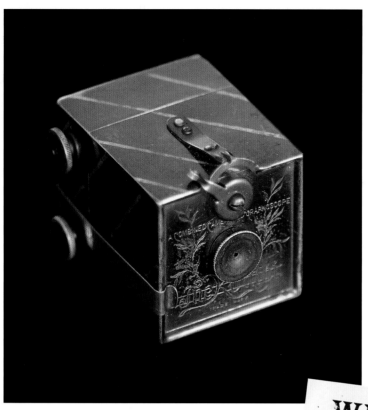

Graphoscope Combined Camera

Patented in 1892 by Alfred Kemper and introduced in 1893, this was the world's first miniature roll-film camera.

Among other firsts, it was the first camera that used film manufactured by Kodak™ solely for use in a non-Kodak camera.

It was also the first camera to combine taking and viewing of photographs in the same instrument—you could actually see what you were snapping.

In addition, it was the first metal-bodied roll-film camera of any size. Kemper claimed it was the strongest camera in the world.

It was certainly a big leap forward for photography and brought affordable picture taking by the ordinary public a step closer.

Listen Online—in 1931!

Wireless On Tap

This advertisement is proof there really is nothing new under the sun! Here is the 1930s equivalent of streaming; just pick up the receiver of your telephone, dial the radio line, and, providing you have paid your subs, you could listen to the best the BBC could offer. Ideally attach a loudspeaker, presumably to the telephone circuit.

Of course, the very name "wireless" now becomes a complete misnomer! The system developed was the same as today, a land-line into your residence and for just 1/6 per week you would receive ninety hours of broadcasting—but you still had to have to have a licence!

We understand Hull was the first to try this innovative radio exchange, but then Hull was often ahead of the game in telecommunications, setting up their own municipal system as early as 1902.

What I am unable to establish is how successful the innovation was, in London or in Hull. I suppose as the cost of radios fell the need reduced. Also, unlike modern phone lines and fibre-optic cables that can handle telephone and broadband at the same time, your phone would be permanently engaged as you listened to your favorite programme!

Secret Agents

Cameras in Ladies' Makeup Cases

If only we could see the photos taken by these 1930s ladies' spy cameras. What would they have been used for? Perhaps a lady detective checking out the shenanigans of a wayward husband? Or a female secret service agent intent on a honey trap with the cultural attaché of a foreign embassy?

Sandwich Box Camera

Probably from the 1920s, this sandwich box contains a hidden camera that is activated by a pull of the cord on the side. We believe it was used by undercover agents to photograph possible troublemakers (as seen by the management) at union rallies.

Making the Ozone Layer

Ozone Maker

This exceptional looking machine from the 1920s claimed to purify the air by sending health-giving "Ozone" into the dwelling houses of the upper classes. Apart from the fact that high levels of ozone are dangerous, the only mechanism appears to be a tray for a "solution" and a fan, but who cares whether it worked or not, this was quackery at its classiest. Worth having in the home just for its looks.

More Tea, Vicar?

Burner and Kettle

This all-in-one water boiler is a self-contained charcoal burner with its own kettle. A sort of elegant British take on the idea of the Russian samovar.

Kettle, Teapot, and Strainer

As if to prove that innovative design, clever use of materials, and good looks are no guarantee of success for the inventor, this electrical integrated kettle and teapot sadly never took off. What a pity; it really is one of the most attractive and ingenious contraptions in the collection. Cup of tea, anyone?

I Need to Go to the "Jennings"

At the Great Exhibition at Hyde Park held May 1 to October 15, 1851, George Jennings installed his "Monkey Closets" in the retiring rooms of the Crystal Palace. These were the first public toilets, and they caused great excitement. During the exhibition 827,280 visitors paid one penny to use them. For their penny they got a clean seat, a towel, a comb, and a shoe shine. "To spend a penny" became a euphemism for going to the toilet. When the exhibition finished and moved to Sydenham, the toilets were to be closed down, but Jennings persuaded the organisers to keep them open, and the toilets went on to earn over £1000 a year. Jennings said "the civilization of a people can be measured by their domestic and sanitary appliances," yet extraordinarily some people actually objected to sanitation, "Visitors are not coming to the Exhibition merely to wash." No, they came not only to "spend a penny," but to comb their hair and have their shoes shined! A veritable spic-and-span bargain!

This example in the collection, with its beautiful flowered glazed printed bowl, is one of the very few left to honour this amazing inventor.

Water Closet

Thomas Crapper—who everyone thought was the original inventor of the WC—was only fourteen when Jennings innovated this toilet. Mind, lavatory humour would never have been the same had it rested on a Jennings and not on a Crapper!

GADGETS FOR LADIES

Almost all the gadgets in this book were invented by men. The Industrial Revolution can appear to be an entirely male world: male inventors, scientists, and engineers reshaped work. Men had the skilled jobs in the foundries and the manufacturing industries, and they dominated banking, medicine, politics, and the law.

The early Industrial Revolution can be seen as entirely negative for women, who left the countryside in increasing numbers for a life of poverty and hard work in the great cities and industrial towns. Yet, later and very slowly, life for many women was changed by invention and technological change, as well as the demands of war in the last century.

As the Industrial Revolution moved into its second phase inventors and manufacturers, still invariably men, turned to mechanising domestic chores. As a result, scattered throughout this collection are items that began to reduce the drudgery of work in the home. From mechanical vacuum cleaners to the early washing machine, from dough mixers to apple parers, gadgets in homes at last began to free women just a little.

With increasing affluence and a little more leisure time, gadgets, gizmos, and knick-knacks were sold specifically to women. This section contains just some of the wide range of fashion and beauty products, from the everyday to the slightly bizarre.

Victorian Ladies' Gun Purse

No, you have not misread the title. Although highwaymen were a thing of the past, footpads, petty criminals, and potential attackers were still a danger in the nineteenth century.

The answer was something straight from a spy novel. Here is an amazing surviving normal purse that has a small gun ready to be fired fitted neatly in the back pocket.

The gun was small calibre and was intended to warn or wound, but not to kill. Nevertheless, it is hard to see the authorities looking too kindly on its use nowadays, no matter the provocation.

Skirt Lifter

The Victorian skirt lifter enabled the sophisticated women of that era to gently pull up the hem of their skirt, allowing them to dance and to walk through muddy streets.

To modern sensibilities, the idea of a Lady's Skirt Lifter, let alone a brand name like "The Grappler," (left) makes us a little queasy. Even in its day, what if the lady grappled too far and allowed rather more leg to show than was seemly for the Victorian gentlewoman!

Holding Down and Lifting Skirts

Thankfully, the Skirt Grappler was not some unpleasant Victorian miscreant, but the answer to a serious problem. In the nineteenth century, dresses and skirts were so long they dragged along the ground. Skirt grips allowed material to be hoisted by hand if the street was muddy or if, for example, you were playing tennis or riding a bike.

Skirt Lifters

Also called skirt suspenders or porte-jupes.

Skirt Weights

To keep the skirt in a fashionable position weights like these would have been sewn into the hem of the material.

Skirt Gauge

By the Edwardian period, it was acceptable for an ankle to be seen, hence this gauge to ensure no more than the ankle would be visible. As a result, the gauge went to six inches and no farther. One can just imagine mamma insisting young Beatrice stand before the gauge before being allowed out, even with a chaperone.

"Am I Undone?"

Zip It Yourself

How would Hollywood have dealt with this latest '50s innovation, a gadget that allows ladies to do up their own zips? It always seemed a part of every 1950s romantic film for the heart throb to be asked coyly, "Oh, could you just help me zip up my dress?"

It might also be seen as a rather sad little invention—perhaps there really was no one to help zip up that party frock.

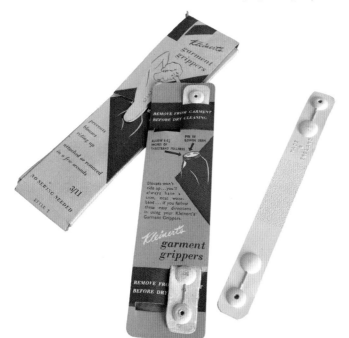

Garment Grippers

To ensure a blouse remained fixed to the skirt, these handy elasticized products would do the job. No crop-tops here, then!

Corset Tester

This one has me beat—why would Victorian ladies want to test for magnetism in their undergarment? It surely wasn't some quackery to measure the magnetism of their personality?

Patting, Piercing, Bustling, and Coshing!

Ladies Cosh

You may well ask, why just for ladies? I have no answer, other than it looks more attractive as an accessory. It would make no difference to the footpad when hit, though.

Face Patter

By bringing blood to the surface of the cheeks, this 1950s rubber sprung device made ladies' faces appear rosier—if not positively flushed!

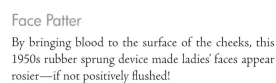

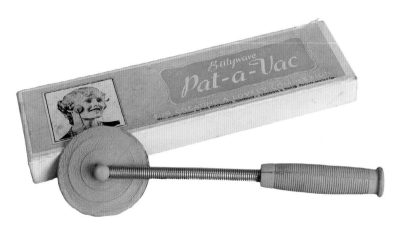

Edwardian Bustle

Fashions of the past must have seemed perfectly sensible at the time, but appear faintly ridiculous to later generations. So it is with the bustle. Here is an Edwardian example. The wire mesh plumped out the skirt at the back. Still, I suppose no dafter than some of the fashions since those times.

Ear Piercer

A less feminine device. We believe this to be a very early instrument for piercing sailors' ears. Painful as this might look, the needle is extremely sharp—we know!—so maybe it was not as brutal as it appears.

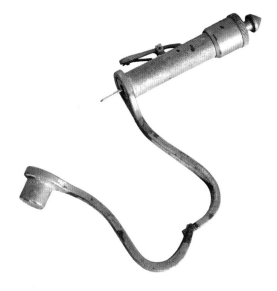

Delightfully Delicate

Calendar/Visiting Card Container

What a lovely idea to take as a small gift to a dinner party or as a little stocking stuffer at Christmas. Quite delightful! This one is for 1874; each year had a new design.

Soap Leaves

Especially in the days of empire the need to carry one's toiletries in a light, transportable pack was a necessity. Here are two examples: the Soap Leaves are pieces of card impregnated with soap in a handy little book; the Powder Leaves are the same idea for talc.

Court Plasters

Waterproof plasters in a handy pocket-sized container, ready for any small cut or abrasion.

The Ladies' Golfing Muffler

The Golfing Muffler

The scarf started out in its modern form in the early nineteenth century. Thicker scarves, designed more to be serious draught excluders rather than a mere fashion accessory, were often called mufflers, a word also applied to the early silencers on car exhaust pipes. This Edwardian gillet is marketed as a muffler—no doubt particularly useful on those bracing east coast links courses!

Girls' Night Out

Lipstick Holder Plus

This neat multi-function lipstick case has a tiny mirror in the side compartment, allowing one to apply makeup and check the look of the lips with just one gadget.

Lipstick Lighter

From the 1930s, another dual function gadget for the busy lady about town; this has a lipstick case at one end and a cigarette lighter at the other. Back in the thirties this would have been a must for most handbags.

Garter Purse

The Edwardian equivalent of today's money belt, yet this innovation brings a smile to one's face, as it appears to require the very unseemliness on the part of the wearer that the neck-to-ankle fashions of the period were supposed to prevent. Nor does this unwieldy way of ensuring your money is safe—by having a purse on a cord tied to a belt on the inside of one's undergarments—appear particularly comfortable.

So if you needed to get at the money for the cab fare, you would have to gently lift the skirt—showing, as the song goes, "a bit of stocking"—whilst frantically endeavouring to undo the button to get at the coins to pay the driver—distinctly unladylike.

Not Seeing the Wrinkles

"It sounds ludicrous, but these simple but effective little patches known as Frownies have been around for more than 100 years and contemporary fans—including Raquel Welch—reckon they're an alternative to Botox. They look like brown paper, but you moisten one side and glue it to your forehead for four hours, or ideally overnight. By stretching out the skin, wrinkles are smoothed when you remove the patch, although the effects might not last much longer than a sojourn down the red carpet." — *Daily Mail*, October 2010.

Frownies

The box copyright is 1889, so this simple little invention seems to have been around for at least 125 years.

The plasters work the same way as the Sellotape method suggested in fashion pages today—one idea that really has stood the test of time.

Eye Mask

From the early part of the twentieth century, this blindfold was intended to allow the lady of the house to get a good night's sleep.

Shielding the Waist

The "Corset Shield"

The Victorian corset is a thing of legend, though in fact corsets from the Regency period were often even more restrictive. What was once seen as an essential fashion garment is now looked on with a mixture of amazement and shame. Throughout the nineteenth century, the corset carefully restricted and re-shaped the figure using tight seams, fabric, bone, metal, and laces. According to period, the closing of the corset was made at the front or back and the length was short or elongated above the hips to suit the fashions of the day.

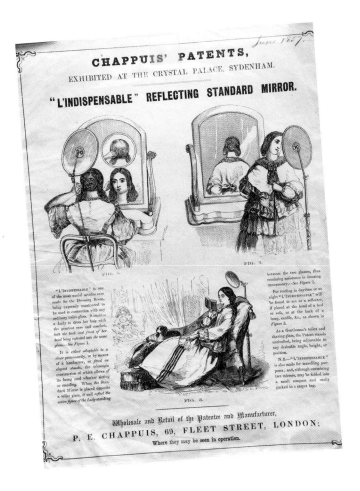

Back Mirror, Back Puff, and Muff Warmer

Back Mirror.

Back Powder Puff

Not so much a back-scrub as a back-pamperer. This one really was for the lady who had everything. A Victorian luxury item.

Muff Warmer

Anyone who has read Victorian novels will know just how delicate was the constitution of young ladies. The slightest hint of a cold and the heroine was in mortal danger. No wonder the Victorians were obsessed with warming clothes. Here, just fill with hot water, place into the muff, and all will be well on leaving the house!

Are You Ready Yet?

Nail Polisher

Polishing nails, thirties style. Just place your fingers in each of the grooves on both sides of the contraption, revolve rapidly, and your nails would be buffed to perfection. A home manicure in no time at all!

Mirror Cleaner for Compact

"I'm just powdering my nose." A euphemism? Not this time. You are powdering your nose, but you can't see your nose in the compact for all the powder on the mirror. A problem has been identified. There must be an ingenious solution, and here it is: each time the device is opened it automatically cleans the mirror. "Won't be a moment!".

Ladies' Hair Restorer

Looking like an implement of torture, this brush's main purpose was to stimulate hair growth. The sales copy claimed it had electrical qualities that added to its hair restoring ability. The idea would be for the plastic teeth to build up static electricity. Sadly, it is doubtful this did more than make the lady's hair stand on end, giving the appearance of greater volume. Of course, as the static leaked into the air, the hair would fall flat again until the next brushing. Perhaps the answer was a portable Van der Graaf generator—now that would make your hair stand on end!

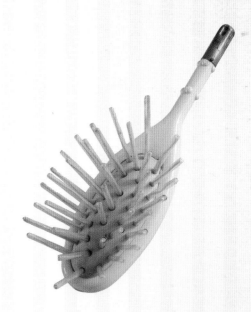

Darn It!

Darning Mushroom

Wooden darning mushrooms have been around a long time. This improved metal version is nothing if not robust. Perhaps it was intended for commercial rather than occasional household use.

Adjustable Darning Mushroom

The type of stitching can be adjusted on this elaborate, clunky mechanical darner. We believe it may have been used for nylon stockings, but we would be pleased if any reader could confirm this.

Automatic Mushroom

The sock is placed over the collapsed darner, you give it a push, and it opens out, ready for the needle. An attractive little household gadget.

Darn, a Ladder

Nylon was first used for fishing line, surgical sutures, and toothbrush bristles. DuPont touted its new fibre as "strong as steel, as fine as a spider's web," and first announced and demonstrated nylon stockings to the American public at the 1939 New York World's Fair. In 1942, nylon went to war in the form of parachutes and tents. Famously, nylon stockings were the favourite gift of American soldiers to impress British women.

Stocking Darners

Stocking darners go back hundreds of years to woollen stockings—long before nylons—yet their use, with kits like this, carried on to repair ladders and tears. Nowadays, of course, a laddered stocking is cast aside without a thought.

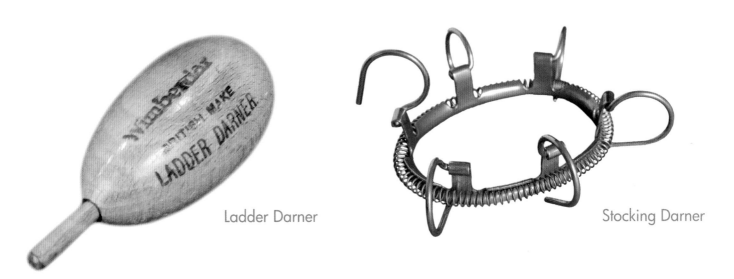

Ladder Darner

Stocking Darner

Mending and Massage

Face, Neck, and Arms Massager

The "Massarger" [sic] has a whiff of quackery about it, playing on eternal worries of crows feet and wrinkles, not to mention double chins!

Hose Mending Outfit

Not sure any lady would want to carry the whole lot of threads in her handbag, but a useful travelling repair kit nonetheless. Ideal for those emergencies when holes and ladders appeared.

Collar Support

The exact use of the support is unclear. Despite the feminine styling and the "Queen" brand name, at first sight it appears to be a man's bejewelled collar connector, but it says it is a collar support, so a collar support it must be—but how did it work?

Popping Pins

Seamstresses and dressmakers used millions of pins and there were scores of devices invented to make getting the next pin that much easier.

Automatic Pin Dispenser

One press releases one pin from this 1930s bakelite dispenser. The pins themselves all lie in the base of the contraption, but a clever design of the internal moulding forces all the pins to lie in one position, so, when needed, just a firm press and—hey presto—up one pops. Just mind it doesn't stab you as it emerges!

Magnetic Pin Watch Holder

The dressmaker would always have pins at hand with this clever and beautifully simple 1920s invention.

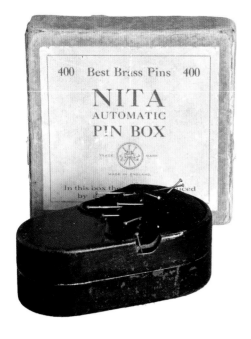

Automatic Pin Box

Another ingenious dispenser. This system relies on magnetism to have one pin follow after another in an amazingly efficient way.

As one pin is pulled up, another is magnetically attracted to the entrance. But the box lid surely has an error—the pins are clearly steel not brass, and brass wouldn't work!

Nimble Thimbles

Adaptation added greatly to the efficiency and usefulness of many everyday objects. Here are two clever adaptations of the simple thimble, both designed to ease the task of the seamstress.

Cotton Cutter Thimble

No teeth needed, nor snips! The cotton was cut on the hook at the end of the thimble with a deft, swift pull on the thread.

Cotton Threader Thimble

Having cut the cotton, one would need to re-thread the needle; the adaptation on the side of this thimble was designed to aid this task. Especially useful to those over a certain age with less than perfect eyesight!

The Eye of a Needle

Needle Threader

Over the years, many have found it difficult to thread a needle with cotton because of poor eyesight, age, or simply lacking the necessary dexterity. So, of all the inventions from the Victorian period—many of them not patented—the needle threader must be one of the most useful. Still today needle threaders are useful gadgets. Here you have one threader that is Victorian and one from the 1950s (the one made of plastic). Sewing machines also needed threading and so here, too, is one produced by Singers to help get cotton through the eye of the needle of the machine.

Pins and Balls of Wool

Ball of Wool Holder

For the Edwardian lady whilst knitting. The ball of wool is skewered by the peg and the whole thing is clasped round the lady's belt, preventing the wool constantly falling to the floor.

Packet of Pins

These toilet pins from the 1920s are beautifully packed in ranked layers—done by machine or by hand (one sincerely hopes by machine)?

Ladies Face Shield

Unlike the twenty-first century, when having a sunburnt skin is the ultimate look in health and vigour, the Victorian and Edwardian ladies—and of course the wish of their menfolk—was to have a pale and pallid look.

This dual collapsible travelling screen allowed ladies to shield their face from fire and sun. It came complete with a natty red travel case.

Off One's Head!

Hair Waxing Machine

Looking like a cross between *Day of the Triffids* and *War of the Worlds*, this variation on the hair dryer sprayed hot wax all over the hair of the client, allowing the stylist to use his / her creative talents to sculpt the tresses.

Paper Curler Holder

Strapped to the wrist of the hairdresser, this canister contained the premade paper curlers required to create the perfect wave. Genuinely handy, these dispensers would see millions of uses, from the Grecian curls of the Edwardian period, through the "Finger Wave" of the thirties, to the "Victory Roll" of the 1940s.

Scent Brush

This brush had the advantage of perfuming your hair while brushing it. You filled the pad with scent that percolated through as you brushed. Only problem was, the "allure" may have been overpowering. Not so much a case of enticing your partner with fine fragrance as asphyxiating them as they nuzzled your hair drenched in Cosby's No. 2 Perfume Essence.

Curly, Wurley Hair

Papillotes

How many hours have we all spent watching Victorian period dramas on television? Who has not been entranced by the wonderful curls and ringlets in the hair of heroines in these dramas? The effect is achieved with the use of paper papillotes, around which small tresses are curled.

So the precise function of these French papillotes of the period is uncertain. Were these lacy items used to hold the papers in place and effect a speedier curl? Can any reader elucidate?

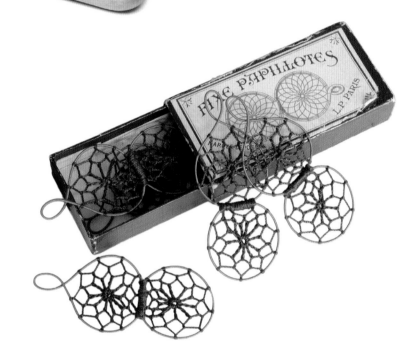

Hair Curler

Still in use today, though now heated and electrical, the hair curler was also used by Victorian ladies. What is unique about this curler is the prongs of the comb retract into the shaft, allowing the curler to be removed without tangling hair—clever and effective.

Yet More Skirt Lifters

In the days of fashionable long skirts there was a real problem keeping the hem clear of mud and dirt on the streets before letting the skirt down to its full length indoors. The answer was a "skirt lifter," like a pair of small tongs suspended by a cord, ribbon, or chain that was attached to the inside of the skirt just below the waist.

Modern historians refer to the object as a skirt lifter, though period sources often used the terms "skirt suspender" or "dress holder." These examples cover a period from 1860 to 1910. There was a wide variety of designs and patents, but as fashion changed and the skirt no longer touched the ground the need for these products totally disappeared.

Garters and Wigs

Inflatable Wig Stand

From the 1950s. We just love the face on the stand— so simplistic. States it could double as a hat stand!

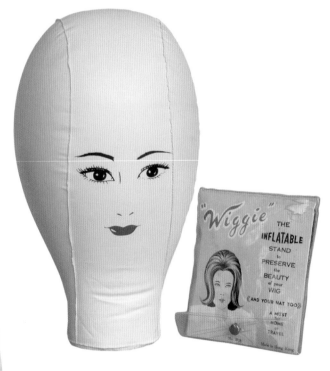

The Celebrity Garter

Having celebrities promote your wares is nothing new. Along with your "Sphere" Oval-Octo garter, you were invited by Dame Nellie Melba to try their suspenders. Looks Edwardian, but the opera singer was only made a dame in 1918, so it is probably from the early twenties.

Patriotic English Corsets!

Hahns Corsets

At first we could not fathom the reason for these advertising cards; there is no date, but the images of the ladies trying on the corsets initially made us think it was from the early 1920s.

The Russian anthem is decidedly pre-revolutionary, and the reverse of the card on the right is the Marseilles, so we now think these flyers must be from the start of WWI, building harmony between the three Allies.

This also fits into the patriotic copy, "Made in England by British Labour." Could it also be the company Hahns proving it was thoroughly British and nothing at all to do with the German Hun?

GENTLEMEN'S CONTRAPTIONS

What could be more opposite? Gadgets were, almost invariably, dreamt up by men, designed by men, and made mostly by men in metal-bashing factories owned by men. And here they are: gentlemen's gadgets for gentlemen.

Many of them are all about shaving; elsewhere there are accessories for the gentleman's wardrobe.

As beards became less fashionable the moustache had its time on the upper lips of men of all ages and classes. Shaving became a daily ritual and gadgets proliferated to make it safer and more pleasant.

The moustache, like the beard, could be something of a nuisance, especially if dining in society. Not only was there the possibility of food spilling from mouths into the thickets of beards, but a healthy moustache could be reduced to a wet flannel by merely drinking tea. Even here, there was an answer—the fail-safe moustache cup—which Edwardian household would be without one?

Pull Your Socks Up!

Boston Garter

From the 1920s onward, this adaptation of the ladies' stocking garter has been keeping men's socks up across the civilised world. Even today there are gentlemen who still use this device to prevent the slightest hint of bare leg or rumpled stocking top appearing beneath a turn-up. A must have item for every gentleman.

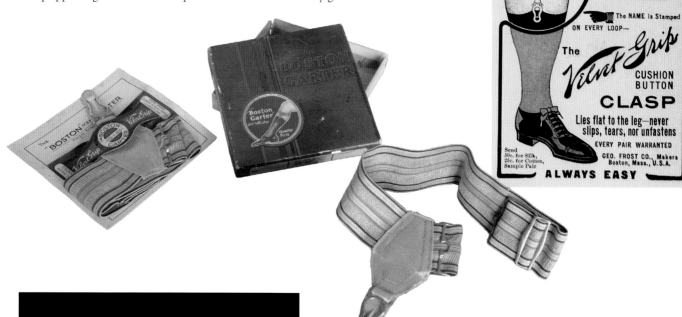

Moustache Protector Cup

This extraordinary cup was designed to prevent one's moustache from becoming doused with liquid as one drank one's tea. The Edwardian gentleman would not have wanted to appear with a stained or sopping moustache. What does one do if one is left handed?

Used Razor Blade Holder

Even a well-used "blunt" razor blade can still be dangerous, so how to dispose of it? Simple, buy one of these pot "frogs." They hold up to 100 blades. Then just throw the lot away and purchase another "frog." Built-in obsolescence from as early as the 1930s.

Being Stylish, Man-Wise

Napkin Holder

This handy portable napkin holder kept the cloth firmly in place to stop the shirt getting covered in food. Just imagine introducing this idea at your local fast food outlet today!

Style Chart and Tie Hanger

A simply wonderful idea! No clashing colours and no outrageous choices of tie with this 1930s style chart. Just set the colour and cut of your suit and you will be advised on the colour of shirt and the tie to wear—splendid!

Sharp Dresser

Tie Presser and Shaper

For the really smart look, this 1930s gadget will keep your tie nicely pressed and the cardboard inners make sure it keeps its shape. Ideal for golf club and old school ties.

Trouser Hanger

This hanger for the wardrobe not only holds the trousers but keeps the crease perfectly with its wide grip.

Crease Maker

These long wooden slats keep those creases razor sharp.

Cardboard Tie Shapers

A 1920s give-away with new ties keeps the diamond shape crisp.

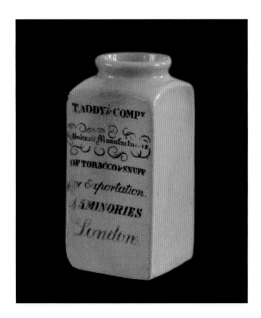

A Pinch of Snuff

Need a nicotine rush? These days, you might turn to e-cigarettes, but well into the nineteenth century, you would have snuffed a pinch of scented ground tobacco into your nostrils. It formed a substantial industry and there were a host of snuff holders of all sizes produced to store it.

Found on shop counters where snuff was being sold, this lovely jar from Tandy and Co would take front place in the display. Transfer printed, it has that quintessential Victorian glistening glaze and intricate lettering.

Honour Snuff Box

This amazing clockwork gadget would also have been found on shop counters where snuff was being sold. The Victorian gentleman would place a penny in the slot and push the plunger, causing the lid to open. He was then "on his honour" to remove only a penny's worth—how many pinches of snuff would that be?

The Conformature

Head Measurer

You might have thought hatters and milliners would just take a tape measure and run it round your head, but to get exactly the right fit for a made-to-measure hat, in the eighteenth century they invented the Conformature. This fine example is made from ebony wood. For precision engineering and craftsmanship, it is on par with a well-made organ of the period. The one at left is made of metal rather than wood and is a late nineteenth century development, but has the same function.

Hats off to the makers of the Conformature!

Hats off!

Hat Brush

A give-away from a clothier, this lovely brush meant you could keep your very natty bowler in perfect condition.

Collapsible Top Hat

What a great invention; the hat collapses to fit into the display box, making it easy to store at home. Then, when you are out at the theatre or the opera, you can fold it up and tuck it under your seat—hence its other name, an opera hat. Beautifully lined, and I would guess very expensive, this French product looks top of the range.

Hat Guard

This 1930s product was intended to keep your boater on in windy weather, but we are not quite sure how it was attached—can any reader help with this one?

It's a Close Shave

Dispensing Shaving Brush

The shaving soap is stored inside the handle of this 1930s patented brush. It is dispensed through the bristles with a press of the button on the end of the handle. Ingenious and useful—no need to keep getting into a lather whilst shaving with this device!

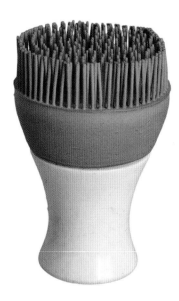

Stubble Softener

The idea was that once the shaving soap had been applied this instrument was used to pummel the face to soften it up for the razor. Don't bristle at this idea—it really works!

Razor and Torch

What a clever idea from the 1920s: a torch with a razor at its business end. Especially when shaving in front of a mirror, and with the light behind you, it gives a really good view of every nook and cranny of even the craggiest chin.

Razor Sharp

Razor Blade Sharpener

Based on the Archimedes principle of the inclined plane, the movement of the sharpener rollers, made of grinding stone, gave a fine edge to the steel of the blade.

Pencil Sharpener

It's very rare to find one of these very inexpensive 1930 sharpeners where the sharpening edge was a normal razor blade that could be easily changed when blunt.

The Sharpest Tool in the Box

Razor Hone

The cutthroat razors of the nineteenth and early twentieth centuries were in continuous need of sharpening. This hone, made of carborundum, would give the very finest cutting edge to the meanest razor.

Rotating Sharpener

Place the blade in the holder and your index finger in the cup and give it a twirl to produce a really fine, sharpened edge—just mind your finger!

Safety Razor Angle Jig

With the normal, everyday twentieth century razor, the resulting sharpness of the blade depended on the angle at which you held it whilst sharpening. This very rare and unusual gadget ensured the correct angle every time.

Top Hat Holder

This patent device ensured your top hat was hung correctly in the Edwardian gentleman's club.

Top ho! No crushed or mangled toppers on leaving in the early hours to hail one's Hackney carriage.

Waiter! I Think There's a Moustache in My Soup

Moustache Spoon

Just the thing for the Edwardian gentleman. Soup could stain a moustache terribly, especially oxtail, and imagine all the bits trapped in the hair from tackling Cullen skunk! Instead, just drop the protector lid into place, scoop up the soup, raise to the lips . . . Oh, and remember not to slurp!

Travelling Moustache Protector

Used when drinking a cup of tea whilst out visiting, this would fit on the rim of the cup, offering upper hair protection. I wonder whether David Lloyd George ever used such a handy protective device when visiting ladies of his acquaintance?

Cutting Edge of Elegance

Folding Knife

A neat knife that has a scissor-type collapsible mechanism, making it easy to carry without damaging your pocket, but take care when you open it! From the 1920s.

Moustache Trimmer and Comb

From the Edwardian period, when upper-lip hair growth was all the rage, this knife was designed to trim and comb the moustache. Just the thing for every suave gent!

Hang 'Em High, Then Crease Them!

Campaign Tent Hanger

In the Boer War, officers went to battle with all the products needed to make them feel like home away from home. This leather belt with its hooks would be placed around the middle pole of the bell tent.

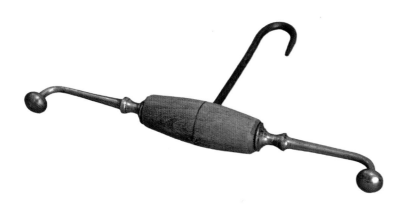

Wig Hanger

Have you ever wondered what happens to the judge's wig after use? Well, it would be on this type of hanger, waiting for the next case. "But where do I hang my Black Cap?"

Tie Hanger

When ties were all the vogue, a stylish man would wear a variety of different ties, each for its own occasion. This artefact would give over thirty varieties to choose from. "Only thirty?! And where are my cravats supposed to go?"

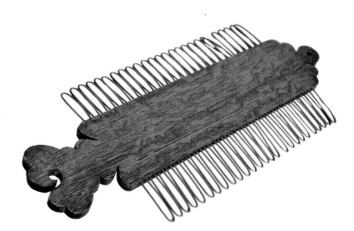

Trouser Hanger

There was a time in the '20s and '30s when having a crease in your trousers was more important than having holes in your jeans! Here is the perfect device to keep everyone in line.

No, You're Winding Me Up!

With plug-in electric shavers still a novelty and modern rechargeable battery shavers a long way off, manufacturers in the mid-twentieth century stuck to clockwork or cord-pull dynamos to give shavers a better deal.

Thorens Clockwork Shaver

The key to wind-up this "easy to hold" implement is at the rear; when the red button is pressed the cutting end whirrs.

Dynamo Generated Shaver

To get a great dry shave the cord has to be continuously pulled to keep the shaver going. You need both hands and great coordination. No wonder so many men stuck to a safety razor.

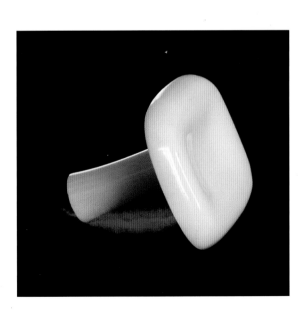

Clockwork Razor

By winding up the base of this shaver, the head, using a normal blade, vibrates to increase smoothness. Rather clever!

Something for the Weekend, Sir?

Shaving Cream Spreader

How to get the cream well into all parts of the beard? Step forward this 1930s device. Also useful upright as an ashtray, a dish for holding hors d'oeuvres, or a minor work by Henry Moore that you happened upon in a gallery the other day.

Collar Shaper

Stiff upper lip? This was aimed more at the stiff lower neck. When collars were worn separately one would pull the collars through the slits so they were curved to just the shape of one's neck.

Boots from the Great War

In WWI, boots were a must at the front. The officers had to keep their position of rank and leather footwear immaculate at all times. The wooden stretchers had to fit perfectly, hence the widening device with the handle. Of course, it was the officer's batman who would stretch the boots night after night.

Sani-Spread Shaving Creamer

This natty folding gadget from 1912 is an aid for spreading shaving cream evenly over a gentleman's face. It seems it was intended that additional softer shaving cream would be placed in the aperture at the top of the implement, giving an even creamier softness to the lather.

Spats

In the days when mud was everywhere—on the streets of towns and cities, as well as on lanes and byways—various ways were found to allow one to arrive at a house in relatively clean boots. Gaiters covering the lower leg and most of the boot were one solution and are still used today by outdoor types, but spats was another.

Spats—short for spatterdashes or spatter guards—were always a more upper-class accessory, and by the time this pair from the late 1920s had been made they had ceased to be a mud-guard and had become a fashion in their own right, though one that by that time was already on the way out.

Also of interest are the very clever three-part shoe trees used to keep the boot in perfect shape.

Altogether—boots, spats, and shoe tree—recall an age of Jeeves and Wooster.

KEEPING IT CLEAN

Housework is still a chore and cleaning jobs are still regarded as menial, usually involving unsocial hours. Yet nowhere has gadgetry and invention helped more in reducing drudgery than in our constant battle to keep our homes and ourselves clean. It has not done away with mops and cloths, but it has reduced the time and labour expended on washing and cleaning.

As the big houses and even the suburban villas found it impossible to maintain large staffs and as the maids and butlers were let go, so machines and innovations took over at least some of the work. The result was significant social change.

The social change for women was particularly marked, though merely producing washing machines and vacuum cleaners has not altered the fact that most housework and many low-paying cleaning jobs are still done by women.

As with many other gadgets, mechanical invention preceded the age of electricity. Hand-operated washing machines and vacuum cleaners may appear archaic or even laughable, but they were steps towards the machines of today, so scrub up, get to work with a bit of spit and polish, and see how, in this area at least, times have changed for the better.

The Metal Posser Pummelling Suction Stick

Suction Posser

One of the toughest jobs going in the past, and still today in many parts of the world, is getting clothes clean. Do you remember the copper posser? It was still seen in Britain even as late as the 1960s, until washing machines became ubiquitous.

This example is a double-cone and uses suction to drive the water through the dirty clothing. The perforations on the inner cone allow the water to circulate.

Metal possers were more suitable for manufactured cotton clothes than earlier tools designed for linen, as only the heaviest cotton fabrics could take a beating from a big wooden dolly.

Spit, Polish, and Benzine

Shoe Brush

What is exciting about this everyday object is the advertising material on the back of the brush; the manufacturer has gone to the trouble of having it printed on tin with bright enamel colours. Probably a give-away—a constant reminder of whose polish to use as you scrubbed those boots.

Dry Cleaning Brush

Made from the 1920s onward, this tank on top of a brush saved lots of time and money by dry cleaning one's garments without rushing off to the cleaners. Based on the use of Benzine—sometimes called petroleum ether or ligroin—the warning on the box was wise, as it is highly flammable.

Flat Iron Cleaner and Waxer

Flat irons may have been flat, but they often stuck to clothes and creased material. The answer was to cover them with a thin film of beeswax to keep them clean and prevent them from sticking. This packet of sheets of waxed paper would be ironed on first before the heavy duty work began.

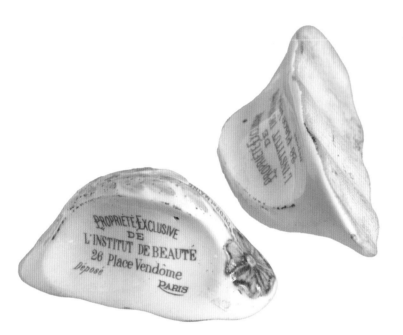

Keeping Clean and Smooth

Hard Skin Remover

The French Beauty Institute produced this attractive hard skin remover as a tool to keep the heel of the foot young and attractive and prevent calluses from developing so the Parisian could walk with total confidence.

Edwardian Shower

No bath? No shower? No problem—the Allen Sanitary Fountain is at hand! Just fill the container with hot water, hang up anywhere in the house, attach tubing between the nozzle in the base and the end of the brush, open the tap on the nozzle, and you are ready to shower. Perhaps best not used above one's best carpet!

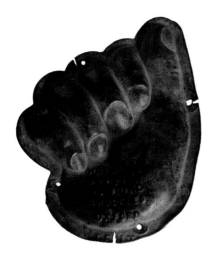

Pummelling the Clothes

Hand Shaped Agitator

This Edwardian wash-day aid looks quite sinister, like some sort of villainous knuckle duster. It was screwed to a board. The idea was you rubbed the wet clothes across it and the fingers acted as ribs, like a scrubbing board—but then why not use an ordinary scrubbing board?

Washing Tub Stirrer

The wooden stirrer had holes through the blade end to make it easier to swish round the water in the tub.

Agitated and All Shook Up

Removing dirt from materials has not changed that much since human beings first recognised the benefits of cleanliness. Still today in many rural communities around the world, the only way is to use rocks and stones by the river's edge to pommel the fabric until the stains are removed. Over the years many patents have been taken out to make things easier, right up to modern washing machines, but virtually all rely on agitation of one sort or another, and the washing board remains one of the enduring symbols of the Victorian era.

Salesman's Sample Washing Machine

The ultimate late-Victorian sales aid. This beautifully crafted model would fit snugly in the salesman's cavernous portmanteau. Not being able to carry around a full-size version of the latest hand-driven, wooden, highly-geared washing machine with its attached mangle, the salesman could instead show off this model and assure the housewife it would transform her life, as well as clean clothes to perfection.

Reverse Agitator

A clever idea from the 1920s, but one that didn't take off. The idea was to improve the effectiveness of the old washing boards by placing the agitating ridges on a hand roller system, but then you still had to hold on to the clothes, so maybe not as clever as it looks.

Wash Day Blues . . .

Hand Operated Washing Machine

It's 1900, and you've just bought the laundry maid the latest thing, a wooden washing machine and mangle. How clever; it contains raised ridges inside the barrel.

All the young maid has to do is turn the handle hard for a long time. Oh, and then put all the clothes and sheets through the mangle, turning again. Yet even this might well have been an improvement on the Dolly Tub and the Set Pot of the old laundries.

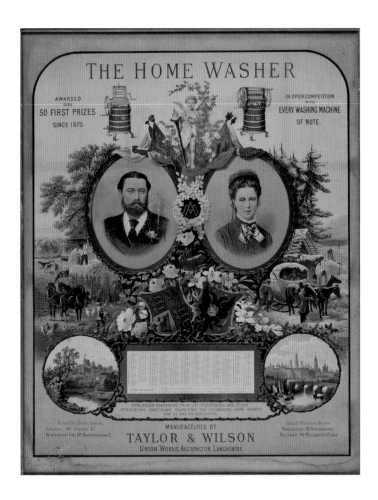

The Home Washer

A beautifully printed Victorian calendar poster advertising "The Home Washer."

I'll Huff and I'll Puff . . .

THE "ZORST" VACUUM CLEANER

In the years between the carpet beater and the broom on the one hand and the electrical vacuum cleaner on the other came machines such as the Zorst. This was a two-man—or more likely a two-woman—operation. One of the servants wound the wheel as fast as she could, thus moving the bellows and creating suction, whilst the other servant used a pipe from the machine to clean the carpet.

The idea was fine, but this could hardly yet be called a labour-saving device. The intention was clear: to automate as much of the drudgery of housework as possible. The Zorst represents the "missing link" in the development of the vacuum cleaner, and, just think, we might have ended up not hoovering the carpet but zorsting it!

The "Star" Vacuum Cleaner

Forget the gym! All you need is this inexpensive 1912 dirt remover. Just push and pull really hard and fast on the handle to develop suction, hold on tight, and drag over the carpet, all at the same time. Nothing to it!

So get those muscles into shape. Give those biceps a real workout. Forget the weights and the dumbbells, all you need is the "Star," a dusty carpet, and a lot of energy.

Then again, you could fork out on a vacuum cleaner driven by an electric motor. Portable domestic electric vacuum cleaners were available from 1907; trouble was, only the affluent could afford them. For everyone else it was still just the broom or the carpet beater, or else a device like the "Star." Broom, carpet beater, or Star, they all needed a lot of sweat, something not always in short supply in 1912.

Another Lot of Suckers

Wheel-Along Vacuum

The beauty of this machine is the action of pushing the cleaner actually activates the bellows, thus generating the suction. Clever, relatively cheap, and versatile.

Car Seat Cleaner

More nearly up to date, this 1950s vacuum brush, powered by batteries, is a very effective little cleaner.

Queen Vacuum Cleaner

Patriotic and effective, "The Queen" cleaner, patented just after WWI, worked by constantly pumping the top sliding handle to create suction. It is remarkably good at removing dust—just jolly hard work for a large room.

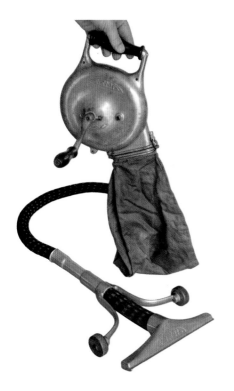

Make Your Own Vacuum

Portable Manual Mini Vacuum Cleaner

Bet you thought hand-held mini dust-busters were a new invention. Not a bit of it! Here is a 1930s device that beats them to it. You held on with one hand and turned the handle like mad with your other hand to create suction. It works, but you do need a rapid wrist movement.

Now, I know what you are thinking: how do you hold on with one hand, turn the handle with your other hand, and use your third hand to direct the wheeled nozzle? We believe it originally came with shoulder straps to free up a hand.

Polishing off the Stove

Cleaning and polishing an old cast iron stove was a routine chore for the maid of the house. Cast iron is sensitive to water, which will create rust, so the old-fashioned cleaning methods using brooms, oils, rags, and stove black were the best. However, the inside of cast iron stoves could be cleaned easily, as cooking drippings simply burned away with each use.

This polish from 1871 claimed it was "always ready and gave perfect satisfaction," and was intended to give the surface of a stove a lustrous shine.

Cleanliness before Even Godliness: The Battle against the Bug

Manganous Carbon Filter

Ever been on safari? Even today in Africa, intrepid travellers boil water and filter it before drinking. Many Victorians were on safari at home and abroad. London and other great cities were jungles of squalor and disease. "Is the water safe to drink?" The answer was "No!" Filtering through charcoal at least reduced the risks. No wonder many households had a manganese carbon filter. Not so much a gadget as a must-have for many.

Lavatory Disinfecter

Imagine if a guest should catch something nasty from the lavatory or a whiff after use. Thanks to the inventive mind of Mr. Crapper the nuisance could be flushed away, but was the bowl spotlessly clean? Here's where Maw's Patent Lavatory Disinfector came to the rescue. Just pop the disinfectant in and a little was dispensed with every flush. The Edwardian housewife could sleep easy in her bed!

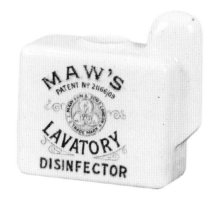

MECHANISING THE KITCHEN

If mechanisation was a help to the chambermaid and the cleaning lady, it was a godsend to the scullery maid and the housewife. Working in kitchens of all sizes, for both men and women, is still hard work, but at least some of the most laborious jobs have been mechanised.

Something as simple as peeling and coring an apple attracted hundreds of different inventions. Other jobs—mixing and scraping, grating, and baking—all had the Victorian and Edwardian inventor working on them. Some of the results appear clunky and over-engineered, but they were the precursors of today's electrical kitchen gadgets.

Many devices were clearly intended for the big house or the kitchens of hotels and gentlemen's clubs. They are cooking on the grand scale. Yet even the ordinary household kitchen saw innovation and smaller labour saving devices.

Still today, the quest for the perfect lemon squeezer or garlic crusher goes on—just look in any well-appointed kitchen shop. Plastic and stainless steel may have replaced cast iron and copper, but the ideas remain the same.

The Norman Churn

How do you make butter? Essentially, you need to keep the cream of the milk on the move, agitating it all the time. This separates the fat from the buttermilk. Simply shaking the cream in a closed jar for an hour will give you the same result, as well as tennis elbow! In ancient times, you swung the unseparated milk in an animal skin, a method still used in some parts of the world, but the Victorian inventor had other, better ideas . . .

Barrel Butter Churn

Turning the handle causes the paddles inside the barrel to turn, agitating the cream and turning it into butter. The French called this a Norman Churn. It was used mainly for smallholdings or homes with a few cattle. This beautifully preserved example is late Victorian.

Mrs. Beeton Comes under Pressure

Pressure Cooker

Mrs. Beeton set the standard for cooking in the nineteenth century. Her book *Household Management* became the bible for Victorian ladies everywhere. Youth was no bar to advancement: Mrs. Beeton was just twenty-five at publication. Nor was she against new technology: she made use of early pressure cookers. Mrs. Beeton had every faith in the weighted spring valve on the lid, yet food could get trapped in the valve and block it, pressure would build, and the cooker would go off like a bomb. Thankfully, Isabella Beeton died in her bed, but sadly at a tragically early age; she was just twenty-eight years old.

We'll Squeeze Them Till the Pips Squeak

Lemon Squeezer

By turning the handle on this bizarre contraption, the ratchet gears caused the top cup to descend inexorably, squeezing every drop of liquid from the lemon.

Lemon Squeezer

A much more industrial looking compressor of lemons, this machine cut the lemon in half and squeezed out the juice at an extremely fast rate, simply by pulling down the handle. All done in a jiffy, so to speak.

The Victorian Bread-Maker, the "Mysto"

Dough Mixer

Back in Victorian days, when fresh bread would have been made in many upper class homes and where the quantities would have been large, a machine to mix dough well and have it ready for proving would have been a godsend. A variety of different designs existed, some with a hot water reservoir at the bottom to keep the dough pliable. The "Mysto" just had a heavily geared mixing end to make life a bit easier for the kitchen maid.

Making More Dough

Dough Mixer

This more elaborate mixer has a chamber at the bottom of the machine which, when filled with boiling water, assists the mixing of the dough and starts the proving process.

Ice Breaker

Ice Cutting Machine

In Victorian times, before the invention of refrigerators and freezers, the only way to keep food fresh was by using packs of ice. The ice was obtained from natural sources, such as frozen ponds or ice fields.

Blocks of ice were sold to the wealthier householders who in turn needed to break it into more usable chunks. That's where this gadget came in.

The steel-spiked wheels did the actual breaking into pieces, but despite the high gearing, plenty of elbow grease would still be needed—yet another job for the cook or the kitchen maid.

Peach Peeler

Three Pronged Peach Peeler

Apple peelers were produced in the thousands; peach peelers are rarer to find. Peach peelers required a lighter mechanism and a different shaped blade. Some manufacturers brought out machines that could do apples and peaches, but the only obvious difference we can find in this machine is the provision of different shaped prongs to fit more easily into the peach. Peeling peaches is a messy business at the best of times, especially if they are fully ripe—washing down the machine afterwards would be a monumental task in itself.

Strip and Peel

Vegetable Peeler

We believe the prime use of this late Victorian invention was to remove the surface skin from potatoes—ideal for those lovely sweet new potatoes straight from the ground—but it could be used for a range of other vegetables.

Bean Stripper

Used for stripping runner beans to a more useful size for cooking. The beans fall down the hopper and as the roller is turned they are cut by the long, sharp blades under the roller.

There is also a view that it could have been used for cutting straws for basket work.

Crusty Old Birds

Bird Roaster

Looking like an innocent bread bin, this French contraption has three hooks on which to hang the poor small birds. The whole device would have been placed in the oven for them to be roasted.

Burnt Crust Remover

What did Edwardian bakers do with loaves with burnt bottoms—throw them away? Certainly not! Here is the answer. Like a large, flat file, this tool was used to rasp away the bits that had caught. Worth every penny to the poor, hard-pressed baker!

Baked in a Pie with Relish

Relish Flyer

A late Victorian promotion of Yorkshire Relish. It claimed to have the largest sale of any sauce in the world.

Automatic Pie Maker

We have not managed to understand how this product works in the manufacture of pies, but we are assured it is a pie press of some sort—can any reader elucidate?

Masticators

Mashing up food to make it more edible and easier to digest for children, patients, or the elderly needed some Victorian ingenuity. Here are two very different examples.

Emulsifier

This large machine might possibly have been used in a Victorian hospital or care home. The machine is well geared, making it remarkably easy to turn the paddles inside the tub that mashed the food.

Masticator

This levered masticator would be used at the table to break up food. You can be forgiven for thinking it might also come in handy for extracting teeth or pruning the roses!

Oysters, Eels, and Oats

Oyster Opener

This machine from the late 1940s was used in Cornwall to open oysters at a pace with one pull of the handle. A variety of wooden moulds were made for different sizes of oyster. This particular machine looks as though it has seen some work—thousands of oysters have passed from sea to plate via this workmanlike machine.

Eel Remover

Looking like a barbaric torture instrument, in fact, this grappling tool was used in Victorian pie and eel shops. It was used to remove the eels from the barrel of briny water. "Now, you'll have a pie and mash with that, sir?"

Oat Masher

Before rolled oats from giant mills were widely available, this serrated roller allowed the housewife to produce oats for porridge or oatmeal for baking.

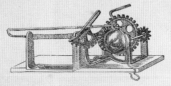

SARGENT & FOSTER'S
IMPROVED
PATENT APPLE-PARER

Sold by **PRATT & CO., 28, 30 & 32 Terrace St., BUFFALO.**

This implement has been in use many years, and highly approved. By the present patent, issued in 1853, the last imperfection was overcome. The ROCKING MOTION, as it is called, given to the knife, makes it a complete machine; and it is the *only one entitled* to use this peculiar principle. The gearing has been improved, so as to act more simply and rapidly, and the machine reversed, so that the right hand is to the crank, and the left to fruit, without obstruction from the machinery.

The peculiar motion of the knife, above named, brings every shape of fruit, whether flat or oblong, perfectly under the control of the cutting edge, be it apple, quince, turnip, or potatoe.

This Parer adjusts itself to the form of the surface, and the knife can be set to take a paring of greater or less thickness, as desired, but always limited and uniform, leaving the fruit in its original shape. The knife being properly set, this machine will save its price in one season, in the amount of the body or pulp preserved, which would be wasted by paring with a common knife. This is an important consideration, especially when it is understood that the most delicate and strong flavor of the apple is in that portion of the pulp immediately under the cuticle or outer skin.

Being well made, and not high priced, not liable to break or get out of order, this Parer must give satisfaction.

Orders solicited, and should be given early to insure supply.

PRATT & CO.

Patent Apple Parer

Although this is not exactly the same parer as shown in the original leaflet, the principle is essentially the same. First patented in 1853, the machine was improved in details over the century, but the same gearing can be found in machines up to the 1930s. There are some domestic needs that hundreds of inventors kept coming back to again and again, and one such is apple peeling and coring. It seemed to hold an irresistible fascination for the Victorian and Edwardian inventor as a problem that needed ever more intricate and wonderful solutions.

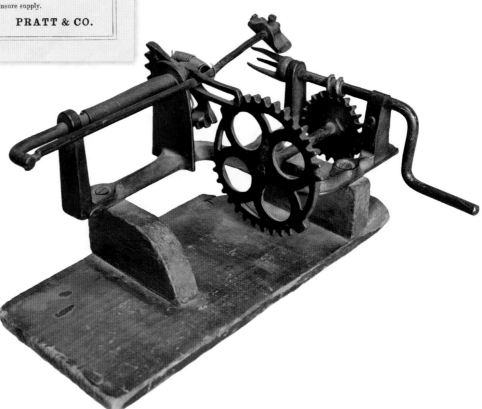

An Apple a Day

Before the 1850s, there was no machine or mechanical aid that would allow a kitchen worker or farm wife to peel apples quickly; this tedious task was performed by hand with a knife. That changed with the labour-saving device invented by David Harvey Goodell, a man who later became the governor of New Hampshire. He called his first invention the "Lightning Apple Parer." At first, a New York firm's marketing efforts sold only 2,400 over two years. Dissatisfied with the outcome, David Goodell took to the road and became his own traveling salesman, and in less than a month he sold 24,000!

Apple Peeler

Patented in 1862, this unusual mechanical apple peeler works on the basis of horizontal motion. Pulling the handle across drives the teethed circular gear, which in turn spins the apple. As it rotates the sharp razor-like cutter takes off the peel as clean as a whistle.

More Apple Peelers

Others copied Goodell. In all over 100 patents exist for the apple peeler, many of which are still in use 150 years after they were invented.

Unicom Apple Peeler

A cumbersome machine to do a very small job, mainly used for industrial peeling for jams, etc.

1950s Apple Peeler

Here is a modern variation on Goodell's original idea.

Doughnuts and Pies

Automatic Doughnut Filler

Have you ever wondered how the jam gets into the centre of the doughnut? Well here is the 1920s answer. The machine is filled with jam, the nozzle pierces the doughnut, the plunger is pressed, and, hey-presto, one jammy doughnut!

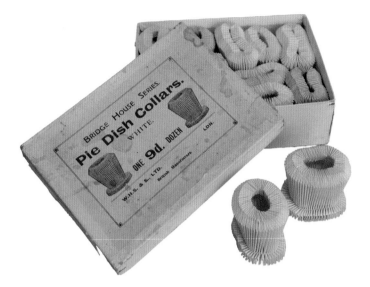

Pie Collars

Made to be expandable, this would surround the finished pie, giving that professional look. Very natty!

Pie Funnel

This allowed steam to escape from the pie, making the pastry light but crusty. Similar funnels are still used today.

Pie Mould

By placing this wooden mould into the dough you have the perfect shape.

Getting Stoned

In the past there seems to have been an inordinate number of patents for cherry stoners. Were more cherries eaten? Was it a much bigger problem back then?

Cherry Stoner

A simple 1920s wire stoner. The cherry is placed on the ceramic disc, the wire is given a hard squeeze, and out pops the stone.

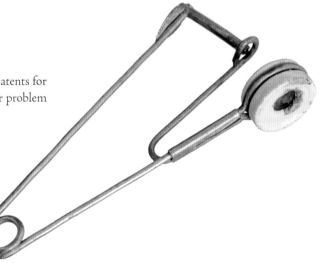

Mechanical Stoner

Late Victorian, and rather clever. Cherries are poured into the hopper. The handle is turned and the business end of the pip remover goes up and down, removing one after another of the cherry stones, and the next unsuspecting cherry rolls into place to be de-pipped.

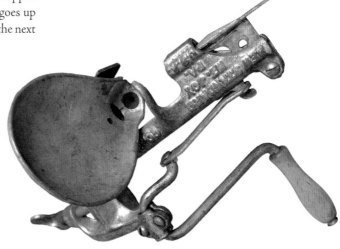

Vertical Stoner

The cherries are placed one at a time into the ceramic holder, the spring loaded plunger is pushed, and out pops the stone.

Cherry Stoner — Four at a Time

Mechanical Cherry Stoner

The Victorian middle classes loved their cherries and inventors loved coming up with ever more elaborate cherry stoners. This one is a deluxe model. By placing a cherry into each bowl of the machine, a quick turn of the handle gives the fastest de-stoning of any Victorian pipper on the market!

Archimedes in the Kitchen

Hand Food Whiskers and Mixers

If you want to do a lot of work, you can either use a big force over a small distance or you can use a smaller force over a larger distance. Archimedes used this principle in his inclined plane screw to raise water on an irrigation project in Egypt thousands of years ago, and it is still in use today in these kitchen gadgets. You push a long way down on the handle and the whisk spins round and does the hard work of mixing the cake. Children's spinning tops work on the same principle.

These early examples vary only in their attachments— which one mixes the best Victoria sponge, I wonder?

French Bird Roaster

The roaster is around three feet in length, so it looks like it could take anything up to a good-sized turkey. Amazingly, it is driven by a clockwork motor that allows the balloon-like bird container to revolve very slowly. The bird is placed inside the wired barrel and is slowly roasted over burning charcoal. An alternative to spit-roasting, and not so very different I suppose from today's hog roast machines. Sadly, the words French and birds suggests to us Brits the slow cooking of our beloved song birds. At least on this occasion we may have to declare our cousins across the Channel not guilty.

Notice that it has two settings: the top one for a faster turn and the lower one for a slower, more concentrated roast.

Why Did the Chicken?

Egg Slicer

Just the job to slice up an egg into wedges for the perfect salad.

Egg Tester

Candling eggs to check whether they are still good is made a little easier with this Victorian gadget.

Egg Weighing and Grading Scales

Egg Boiler × Eight

There you are out in the bush, building a railway or on manoeuvres. All you have is a campfire and a lot of hungry men demanding their breakfast—a perfectly cooked boiled egg. Here is the answer. There are forty men—umm, how many boilings?

Well, Stone Me!

Butter Maker

Looking like a modern sculpture, this is one of the most attractive gadgets in the collection. Better still, this nineteenth century miniature butter churner still works today. I wonder what dairy maids would have made of it? They would have laughed at its small scale and probably thought it a bit flimsy. After all, butter churning was one of the longest and most tiring chores on the farm or in the dairy. Fancy a go?

Cherry Stoner

Automated double cherry stoning was certainly the last word in the Victorian kitchen for efficiency. The cherries are popped in two at a time. Down comes the stoning prongs, removing the stones which fall through the holes, and the fruit is removed as the prongs return, sliding off into the waiting bowl along with the juice. Hand and eye coordination is essential, otherwise it could be your two little fingers being stoned. Would the blood be noticed among the cherry juice?

Cucumbers and Corkers

Cucumber Slicer

A very rare item, so simple and yet effective. It attached to the kitchen workbench with the blade facing upwards. You then struck the cucumber across the face of the blade. But mind those fingers!

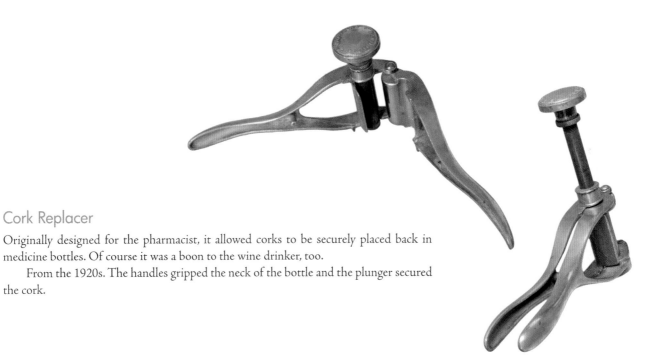

Cork Replacer

Originally designed for the pharmacist, it allowed corks to be securely placed back in medicine bottles. Of course it was a boon to the wine drinker, too.

From the 1920s. The handles gripped the neck of the bottle and the plunger secured the cork.

Meat and Two Veg

Potato Scraper

Place your spud alongside the grating edge, turn the handle, and the peel is removed. Then your potato is ready to make perfect English chips: none of your thin and lanky French fries!

Also useful for removing your skin with one quick turn of the handle. By the look of it, a device much loved by the makers of Elastoplast, which made its first appearance in 1896.

Pea Podder

A very rare example from Victorian times. This machine could strip the peas from their shells in double-quick time. Just fill the wooden container, turn the handle, and out pop those succulent green peas. A real labour saving device. On an industrial scale it founded an industry—first tinned, then frozen peas.

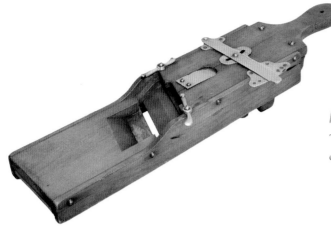

Meat Slicer

To cut your latest gourmet steak into tender slices, the Edwardian chef would run the slicer up and down for the perfect thickness.

Coffee Roaster

Clockwork Roaster

The near-addiction of large parts of the population with coffee is nothing new.

The Victorians enjoyed their coffee, and this little home clockwork roaster would have been used in middle-class kitchens.

You simply wind up the clockwork mechanism, set it to the speed you require, place the coffee in the barrel, light the burner underneath, and then sit back and watch the barrel slowly rotate, savouring the rich aroma as the coffee beans are roasted to perfection.

Save the Bread

and the

Bread will save you

Four-fifths of our Wheat comes from Over-Seas.

German Submarines seriously reduce the supplies.

By taking

2 ozs.=one thick slice

of Bread per day less than you used to take, and AVOIDING WASTE, you will help to defeat the Germans.

ON YOUR HONOUR!

F.E.C. (Scotland) 1.

How Do You Like Your Loaf?

WWI Propaganda Poster 1917

We tend to think of rationing as something from WWII and the late forties, but getting wheat from Canada for bread was dangerous in 1917—German U-boats lurked in the Atlantic—so cutting back on bread was vital. Actually, four pounds of bread a week sounds quite a lot, but bread was even more of a staple of the diet back then than it is now.

Bread Knife Sharpener

This would keep the bread knife razor sharp. Now, do you want your loaf thin or thick sliced?

Bread Slicer

The Edwardians had a solution to the problem of cutting your loaf as you like it. Here is the loaf slicer. Ideal for cottage loaves, bun loaves, and tin loaves.

Vicious Tools for Kitchen Jobs

Tin Opener

Edwardian—once again, mind the fingers!

Ten Tools in One

The proud boast of the 1940s manufacturer is that it had ten uses: tin opener, corkscrew, bottle cap lifter, bottle stop wrench, measure, hammer, glass cutter, paper pattern and stencil cutter, coin tester, and glass breaker.

Wow! But also why? What fiendish mind considered these the ten most valuable tools to be consolidated into one gadget? And what market was it aimed at—the chef with a penchant for smashing window panes, or the glazier who liked his booze?

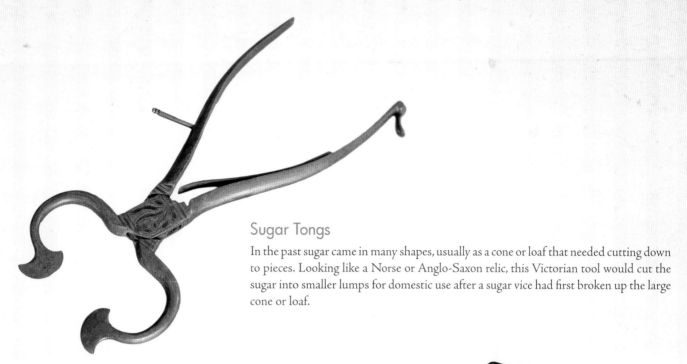

Sugar Tongs

In the past sugar came in many shapes, usually as a cone or loaf that needed cutting down to pieces. Looking like a Norse or Anglo-Saxon relic, this Victorian tool would cut the sugar into smaller lumps for domestic use after a sugar vice had first broken up the large cone or loaf.

Chop, Chop

Vegetable Chopper

A fascinating Victorian apparatus for chopping up vegetables. Each turn of the handle raises four levers with highly honed knife edges at their bottom end. They move in turn, slashing the vegetables into tiny pieces. Ideal for carrot and turnip to go with those chops and kidneys of which the Victorians were so inordinately fond.

Spoon Strainer

We can only assume the particular use for this spoon was to strain vegetables from a boiling pot. The interest lies in the two sections, with a straining sheet between the two sides—how did it work? Has any reader the answer?

Master Chef, 1890

Vegetable Chopper

Looking like a Trevithick steam pumping engine, this was the Victorian answer to the food processor. Turning the handle caused the metal container to turn at the same time the chopper went up and down inside, cutting the vegetables into small pieces. A boon for the busy cook, but a bit of a pain when it came to washing up.

Fork Cleaner

A very unusual kitchen tool that could be adjusted to the space between the prongs. It cleaned the metal spears of forks from unused food, presumably just before washing. It is dated around the turn of the twentieth century, but it was not a commercial success. Like many inventions, a great solution for a problem that didn't really exist.

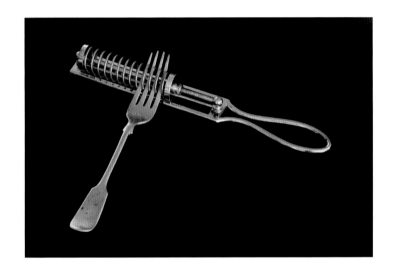

Pudding Basin

Looks like the Lord Mayor's pudding basin was aimed more at the novice cook if the instructions on the side of the bowl are anything to go by:

1. Tie cloth over pudding basin
2. Immerse in pan of boiling water
3. Lift basin off pudding at table
4. Grease all parts well

Was it used at table for the Lord Mayor at Guildhall? One would think the steaming pudding would have had its basin lifted in the kitchens and the pudding presented on a silver platter.

Lick This!

Ice Cream Maker

We were a little stumped as to what this could be at first, and were astonished to find this beautifully finished ceramic ware was, in fact, an ice cream maker. Made by Doulton in the 1890s.

Beauty in the Kitchen

Food Processors

Good design, especially in the kitchen, is not a modern phenomenon. Here is an Edwardian multipurpose food processor—the original forerunner of the modern-day mixer and grater—beautifully crafted in wood and metal. The attachments are drums of different gauze size. Easily changed, they allowed anything from rough cut to nearly liquefied. The power to drive this most attractive gizmo is, of course, "muscle power." Electricity in the home was still in its infancy. With its fine design, this processor may well have been aimed at the rapidly expanding middle classes, where the kitchen would be upstairs not down and there might be a maid but no cook. This might well have been one device turned by the lady of the house.

WHAT A SPECTACLE

Here is an area for flights of fancy and serious gadgets to help people with failing or poor eyesight. The "test yourself" kit is a good example of a device that brought a bit of a better life to people in remote communities.

There are also reminders of just how difficult life could be when ill health and long periods in sanatoria were common. The prismatic glasses enabling one to read comfortably whilst perhaps paralysed in bed are a good example.

Magnifiers of various sorts were also developed. Some were a success, while others appear outlandish or, as with the "third hand," extraordinarily difficult to use. Magnifying glasses are still important today for many older people for whom glasses no longer help.

There are also very clever methods to produce 3-D images from 2-D photos. These early novelties and more serious projectors were for entertainment—more serious use of projectors came later. So, take a look inside . . .

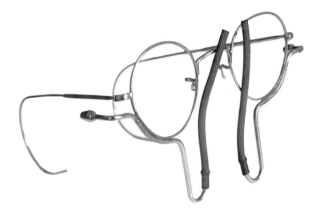

Specs!

Breathing Spectacles

Used in hospitals in the late 1930s to allow patients to read at the same time as receiving oxygen. The rubber nosepieces would be inserted into the nostrils and the oxygen lines from the cylinder were attached at the sides.

Protective Spectacles

These specs appear to have been designed to assist in the ability to see in strong light. Probably from the 1920s, they may also have been used as an extra protection from sparks from machinery.

Extra Magnifier Spectacles

Essentially a magnifying glass to be used with glasses. By attaching these lenses to the bridge of the spectacle frame an area of print can be magnified, making a newspaper or the novel easier to read. The frame is typical of the 1950s.

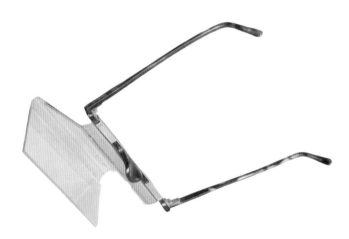

Lighting the Way

Self-Raising Parrifin Lamp

A lovely looking late Victorian lamp. Its added benefit is the base slides into the slots in the travelling box, raising it to a height most convenient for you to read or even for a surgeon to operate.

Spectacle Torch

No, this is not an early mockup of Google Glass. From the 1930s, this wonderful idea allows one to see under the bedclothes if needed, or to read a book in a darkened room. Of course, perhaps it is the inventor who should have gone to lie down in a darkened room—it never took off!

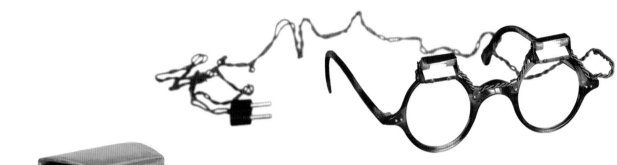

Motorcycle Lamp

Lucas was the main manufacturer of lamps for virtually all vehicles on the road in late Victorian and Edwardian times. This lovely example is ready for use, looking as if it has just been purchased and is straight out of the box. A spiffing example from a spiffing era of motoring.

The Mystery of the "Third Hand"

Third Hand Magnifier

What a simple but wonderful concept—your "third hand." I guess it could have been called the "third eye," as the idea of these finger magnifiers is to allow you to see more clearly without having to use your hand to grip the magnifying glass, thus leaving both hands free. Here you have the same solution—both patented—but the difference is the way the invention grips the fingers and the design of the joint allows the glass to swivel.

The red box is a bit posher because it comes with a small pouch to carry the tiny magnifier in your pocket or purse. Both from the 1920s.

Opening One's Eyes

Expanding Binoculars

Originally used by the army in the late nineteenth century, these expanding binoculars fit easily into an officer's pocket.

Later, the manufacturer advertised them to the public and they became very popular at sporting and hunting events. Ideal for following the gee-gees on the flat, over the sticks, or out on the chase.

Indian Summers

Glare Protectors

Top of the range cool shades for the Victorian lady or gentleman. These spectacles, called glare protectors in their day, were made by famous Indian opticians Lawrence and Mayo, who are still going strong today. The glasses protected the eyes from the hot Indian sun. It is claimed that Queen Victoria used them, and there is a charming photo of Queen Mary wearing these shades on the company's website.

Avert Your Eyes!

Eye Caps

The use of these caps to shade the eyes back in the Edwardian period seems bizarre, given that most lighting was still from candles and oil lamps, so to be protected seems a need that did not have to be met.

Where they were used was in the editorial offices and typesetting rooms of newspapers. No 1930s film involving gangsters or journalists was complete without the hero editor-in-chief sporting black eyeshades and gold armbands on the sleeves of his shirt.

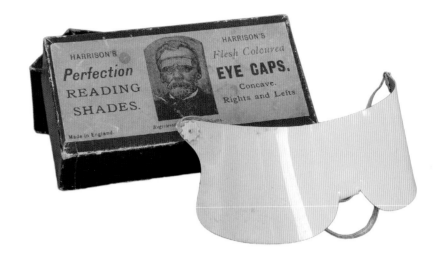

Eye Covers

Where eye protection did make complete sense was in the heavy engineering industries. These metal mesh eye guards were an important safety precaution and reflect the increasing role of safety legislation for workers at the turn of the twentieth century.

Look Here!

Many are the inventions aimed at making reading more comfortable or getting over the problems of increasingly poor eyesight. Some, like magnifying spectacles, are still very useful for watchmakers or model engineers. Others have gone the way of so many inventions over the years …

Magnifying Broach

Attached to a slim metal chain, this very neat little magnifier was for the lady who needed to see better for fine work.

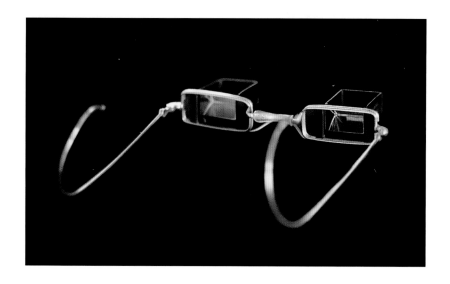

Laying Down Glasses

These clever spectacles allowed you to read whilst lying flat on your back—great for watching television in bed, but used instead by those immobilised by illness. They come from the 1930s, a time when many people spent weeks, months, or even years in sanatoria with crippling conditions such as polio. One such was future Prime Minister Alec Douglas-Home, who was diagnosed with spinal tuberculosis in 1940 and spent two years flat on his back encased in plaster, during which time he read voraciously —perhaps with a pair of these glasses.

Just Looking — All Angles Covered

3-D Postcard Projector

Merely by having a curved mirror in the base, this natty projector makes any postcard into a 3-D picture.

The effect is surprisingly realistic; not quite an early version of virtual reality, but certainly an attempt to make photography ever more vivid and life-like.

Sports Glasses

These binoculars attached to a spectacles frame to bring the action closer, especially at the race course.

Test Your Own Eyes Scientifically—Save $10.00 or More

DIRECTIONS

NU-WAY OPTICAL CO.
29-32 Melinda St.
TORONTO, ONT.

Be Your Own Optician

Eyesight Self-Tester

Used world-wide, this mail order kit allowed you to test your own eyes, write down the prescription, and send away for your glasses. Originally intended for rural farming communities in America in the early part of the twentieth century, this kit was a real boon to anyone living out of reach of an optician. One of many genuinely useful mail order products.

Please Don't Inform on Me!

"Persons finding themselves in possession of these glasses are requested to hand them in to a police constable or deliver them to a police station."

Theatre Binoculars

What is so fascinating about these particular theatre glasses, apart from the fact they give excellent magnification, is the wording on their brass handles:

> £5 to £20 reward will be paid to any information to conviction for persons to be found in unlawful possession of these glasses.

These glasses were hired out to theatres across the country from a company called U.A.D.C. Ltd, which operated a national reward system.

This would have been in the heyday of music halls, late Victorian and Edwardian.

The question is—are you going to tell?

WE ARE AMUSED

Few of us can get through life without a little entertainment. In the past this would have been beer, wine, and song, fiddle music, dancing, and tales told round the fire. The explosion of manufacturing in the nineteenth century gave inventors and entrepreneurs their chance to amuse the public with gadgets of every sort, from the frivolously diverting to the seriously tasteless.

If people need bread and circuses, this part of the collection is the "Big Top." Many of the ideas appearing here are still being peddled today. Some have been big sellers, whilst others have amused a few but lost their promoter a pretty packet.

Manufacturers of more serious products also used entertainment, as they still do today, to promote their wares. Thus was born the free give-away and the promotional pen. The ingeniousness of the advertisers is hardly matched by the electronic wizardry of today's marketing.

It may be Queen Victoria never actually said, "We are not amused," yet her subjects and those of her successors wanted to be amused. They may have been taken in by gimcrack articles or the latest gimmick, but not all their pennies will have been wasted, for you, like they, may well find something to laugh at.

What the Butler Saw

3-Dimensional Postcard Viewer

An elaborate Edwardian piece of entertainment, yet the science behind it is simple enough. The idea was to turn the one-dimensional view on the card 3-D.

The framework at the back of the viewer is to hold a cloth covering to stop light getting in and spoiling the image.

It works by having a curved mirror that seems to do the job. Sadly not perfect but enjoyable to use, though one wonders whether it was worth all this contraption merely to see that postcard of Scarborough from Aunt Ethel in more than one dimension.

Well Blow My Nose and Shake My Bones!

Echophone Organ

An attempt to jump on the band wagon of the popularity of the mouth organ, the Echophone was produced by Hohner to add extra *volume* to their sales—get it?!

Mutoscope

Better known to many as a "What the Butler Saw" machine, the Mutoscope was one of the first photographic motion picture viewers.

Usually the films were only very slightly racy, as in the title of the one showing in this Mutoscope, *Naughty But Nice*.

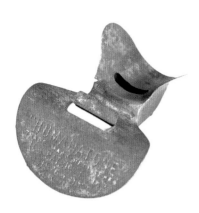

Clakker Bones

The Victorian busker was adept at making music from just these two bones in the hope of a penny—go on, sir, a half-penny—surely you can spare a farthing, lady? In fact, clakker bones were also at the heart of many a Victorian musical hall act—ah, simple pleasures.

Nose Organ

No, seriously, just don't have a bad cold before performing. Place one's head into the device, blow with the mouth and nose, and this late nineteenth century instrument opens up a whole new world of musical novelty.

Clockwork Music Spoon

This is such a lovely idea: just wind it up before feeding time, and then every time baby takes a spoonful, the movement of the spoon triggers a tune. Or you can press the switch at the top to start the tune yourself. All to encourage little Harry or Harriet to have some more. Well done!

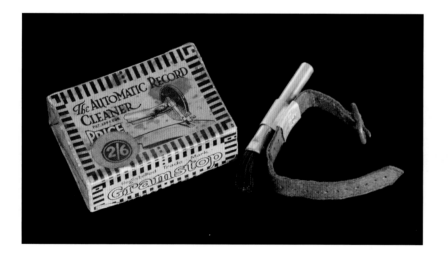

Listen to This!

1920s Record Cleaner

This cleaner would be fixed by the leather belt to the arm of the gramophone and would sweep away any dust ahead of the needle.

1950s Record Cleaner

The Red Edison

The phonograph was invented in 1877 by Thomas Edison. Other inventors had produced devices that could record sounds; Edison's phonograph was the first to reproduce the recorded sound. His phonograph originally recorded sound on a tinfoil sheet phonograph.

This is an absolute gem; the very idea of being able to record and play back one's voice would have been novel enough—the giant horn just added to the magic.

Sound Training

Ventriloquism Teacher

The sad thing is, I purchased one of these as a lad in the late forties—never mastered the technique, alas, so I never got to speak for Lord Charles! The key to throwing the voice lies in the reed, which you put under your tongue.

Bagpipe Trainer (Chanter)

Still used to teach fingering on bagpipes. Bagpipes are essentially a reed instrument, with the bag acting as a reservoir of air. The chanter is a lovely musical instrument in its own right, producing a delicate range of sound. Indeed, some may prefer it on its own.

Turning over a New Leaf

Mechanical Page Turner

The Victorian musician had a number of these mechanical page turners from which to choose; this one is perhaps the cleverest mechanically. It all works by springs. The slightest touch on the lever turns the sheet.

There are, however, drawbacks. First, the sheet music has to be prepared before the concert begins, each page being carefully fitted into the contraption. Then the springs have to be pulled into position. Finally, apart from the noise of the spring going off, there is the possibility of accidentally hitting the lever twice—before you know it you have gone straight from the adagio to the rondo, having skipped the minuet entirely!

Making Faces

Such a simple idea to get the kids interested in developing their artistic ability, perhaps moving them on to portraiture. Most of the silhouettes shown as examples look like a cross between Jane Austen's Lady Catherine de Bourgh and Charles Dickens's Miss Havisham, but as long as the child did not let on that the silhouette was actually of Granny it would make a wonderful birthday present.

Theatre at Home

The Praxinoscope

This amazing and beautifully made French home theatre called the Praxinosope entertained with a very short story on a cardboard printed strip. This was mounted around the multi-mirror, which, when turned, gave the impression of movement and characters on a stage. Unfortunately, as the strip was very short—just the circumference of the outer ring—you really couldn't develop a plot!

Keeping the Kids Happy and Asleep

Cradle Springs

What a great idea—why don't we still have this easy "get to sleep" gadget?

Puppets on a String

In the '50s, these inexpensive card puppets were a cheap and cheerful entertainment for children of all ages. The first one, Miss Britain 1951, has to be seen as an object of its time and taken in that spirit—it would be hard to justify today. It was produced as a memento of the "Festival of Britain." The laughing policeman is also from that period. It was sold as a tourist souvenir in London. Its concertina folds made it a really fun little present to bring back from a trip to the capital.

See the World

Sculptoscope

Increasing footfall—attracting more people into your shop —was just as much a concern for the Victorian and Edwardian retailer as it is on today's High Street. This novelty slide viewer was just one of many ways to attract customers. It would be placed near the entrance to the store and played on the curiosity of the public to see the world long before the Internet and intercontinental air travel.

Just Tasteless

We try not to have unpleasant or tasteless things in the collection, but they were produced and are part of social history, if one we find difficult to comprehend now.

Dancing Figure

Crude representations of African American figures were remarkably common right up to the '50s. Their racist vulgarity is now hard to ignore. Sadly, this 1930s tap dancing minstrel actually is an example of a major advance in the development of electrical toys. When the machine is turned on the membrane vibrates, just like a loudspeaker. By lowering the minstrel on to the membrane, the vibrations are passed into the legs and he starts to "dance."

"Cutie" Table Lighter

Seriously tasteless. Millions of these sort of sleazy and frankly rather crude trashy items were made after WWII. Many of them, like this one, were made in Japan as it tried to rebuild its industry. As a result, it took some time for Japan to overcome the idea of its manufactures being nasty and cheap—not a problem it has today.

Hat Doffing Clown

A more innocent little toy. These simple mechanical brooches were all the rage in the 1930s. They were placed in the buttonholes of the lapels of jackets, and, when the cotton was pulled, the clown doffed his hat to the amazed onlooker.

Turn, Turn, Turn

There were chart wheels (volvelles) for nearly everything, from school subjects to music lessons.

Pear's Give-Away

You can establish what day falls on any date of the year over a sixteen-year period. Pears Soap was one of many companies who used chart wheels as yet another advertising gimmick to establish that all-important brand name.

Guide to the Guitar

From the 1930s, this simple rotating guide assists you to play the Spanish guitar at home. It doesn't seem that long ago that using these printed volvelles was a major part of many tutorials, especially self-help courses.

Keeping One's Cool at the Theatre

The Programme which Turns into a Fan

The Victorians and Edwardians never missed a trick when it came to advertising; not an inch of free space was left unused.

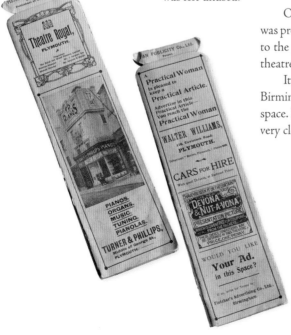

Over 100 years ago, this delightful programme for a theatre in Bournemouth was produced. Unfold it and inside contained the cast list, scenes, and an introduction to the play. Turn it inside out and it revealed this amazing paper fan, allowing the theatre goer to keep cool throughout the performance.

It also gave extra revenue to the theatre; the publisher, Fletcher's Advertising of Birmingham, paid to give away these programmes and made money selling advertising space. Fletcher's own sales pitch was "the programme that would have been kept"—a very clever ploy!

Blow Hard

Harmonica and Bell

The extra instrument on this harmonica—the bell—gives it added interest. From the Edwardian era and beautifully mounted in wood, you can still get a good tune out of it.

Flutophone

The very cheapest so-called harmonica made of a single piece of tin, yet claiming it would play the finest songs. It was a mid-'20s novelty that would have been sold to folks desperate to sing the blues.

Mechanical Postcards

Mechanicals are postcards with moving parts. Usually the printer would die cut the images and they would be put together by hand. They were more expensive to produce but always made an impact with the recipient.

Cheeky Lady

When you see the serene, attractive, bejewelled young woman reflecting shyness and innocence, you do not expect a rather simplistic red tongue to stick out if you pull the tab—the height of frivolity, Edwardian style!

Gambling Man

Hard to figure out the message of this card, but my guess is the sender is inferring he played the tables and lost, as seen by the second figure showing his empty pockets.

Moving Heads

Crazy Face Cards

If you wanted to make someone happy in the late 1930s, just mail them a note on this wonderfully diverting yet ultimately childish rotating wheel card—just like some of the latest apps on our iPhones™. How many different faces could be made?

Heads Up

A clever little advertising gimmick for mustard; just press the tab on the side and the newest little convert to having mustard on their chops pops up.

The Flex-A-Tone

Introducing a new instrument in the world of music is a chancy business—after all, most methods of hitting, strumming, blowing, and plucking have been thought of already. But here is a brave attempt, probably from the 1930s, when jazz was still the rage worldwide

The sound is similar to a hotel bell, sadly, and not the stimulating tone indicated on the box.

Pocket Folding Stereoscope

This amazing pocket entertainer was produced around 1920. By placing the special photographic paper slides into the viewer you could see a remarkably good 3-D image. The viewer came with some picture stories, but sets could be bought separately. The whole thing is so ingenious, especially the way it folds neatly into its tin box. Handling this artefact is a pure joy.

HOUSEHOLD HARDWARE

Is there anything more pleasant, especially on a wet, cold, blustery day, than spending an hour just poking about in a really good hardware store? There are bits and pieces for jobs you have always meant to get round to, gadgets for jobs you would never dream needed doing in the first place, knacky solutions to tricky problems, and, of course, the everyday essentials to keep the house running.

Here is a hardware shop of the past 150 years; there are bits and pieces for jobs all round the house. As the years go on the gadgets tend to get more sophisticated and less clumsy, but their use is much the same.

One area that appears to have vexed inventors is security. The collection includes several door alarms—most of them clockwork—that came well before our modern alarms and infrared sensors. Most of them relied on a wedge under a door which, when dislodged, triggered a loud bell. Did they result, I wonder, in as many false alarms as we are used to today?

So enjoy a browse through a hardware store of the past. Decide on a trivet for the hearth or the best knife sharpener, or that perfect mousetrap!

I'll Ask the Maid to Do It

We would think inventions in Victorian times would have been designed to cut the cost of living for even the better-off households by reducing the cost of servants, enabling the lady of the house to take on many of the everyday chores, or at least by reducing the number of servants by providing novel labour-saving devices. Not a bit of it! Perhaps because of the status afforded by having servants and maids, many of these new devices were marketed not at cutting costs directly, but at increasing the efficiency of the employed staff to free them for yet more work.

The size of the market was staggering; the census of 1891 gave the number of those in service at nearly 1,400,000 females and just over 65,000 men, and this to serve an overall population of just 30,000,000 inhabitants, plus thousands of youngsters between the ages of ten and fifteen. Many worked in the great households of that period, but, increasingly, even lower-middle class families had live-in domestic staff: a much sought after symbol of improving social status.

The conditions for those in domestic service were often poor, usually living in a tiny room at the top of the house, many having to share, and at the beck and call night and day of their employers. Of course, economic circumstance often forced families to send their sons and especially daughters into service; the living-in position often bettered the home from which they came.

As the years passed conditions improved, and the Great War of 1914–1918 wrought great change in the position of women; they were needed to help in the factories to replace the men at the front, which in turn helped women attain the vote in 1918.

Here (left) is a knife cleaner and sharpener called "the servants friend" that would have been used in stately homes. As can be seen by the soap flyer (right) showing the mistress of the house overseeing the use of the cleanser by her maid, marketing was aimed at the householder. These images of employers lauding over their servants abound in sales literature of the period for most products and even for the new "labour saving" devices. They were selling to the employer after all, not the employee!

Knife Sharpener

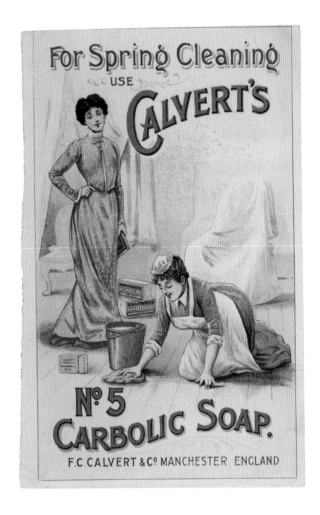

Calverts Carbolic Soap

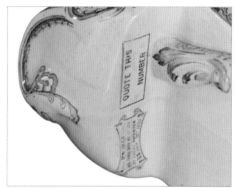

Fresh Every Morning

Patented back in 1891, this beautiful decorated ceramic water container entitled "Royle's Patented Toilet Aquarius" had a specific use; the Aquarius would be found alongside a basin in small hotels or bedrooms where plumbing did not exist. The landlady would have it filled every morning. When the tenant or visitor wanted to wash, a gentle tilt of the Aquarius allowed water to pour into the basin. The waste water had a less lovely receptacle: an old pail under the basin. The Aquarius was invented by Mr. Royle from Manchester, who also created the self-pouring teapot.

Toilet Aquarius

This fine example was manufactured by Royal Doulton, a company better known for tableware and collectibles. Doulton was founded in London in 1815, but, having moved its operations to the Potteries, its reputation grew, even though it was a latecomer compared to Royal Crown Derby, Royal Worcester, Wedgwood, Spode, and Minton.

Stands and Trivets

Trivets were originally used at the hearth; later on they came to be used on the cast iron stove top and then as table protectors, teapot stands, or plant pot rests. They are sometimes referred to as "stands," although that term is more commonly used to describe trivets used as pressing iron (sad iron) rests.

Gas Stove Stand

Claiming to save 50% off your gas bill by doubling the efficiency of your burner by spreading the flames and preventing food in the centre of pots burning. They clearly weren't expecting any inflation—the price is cast in metal!

Sink Or Table Stand

Made of steel and beautifully engraved.

Expandable Trivet

What's so lovely about this metal expandable stand is the way it all fits into one single, compact unit. Available for one, two, or three irons as needed for the larger family laundry room!

Pressed and Hung

Trouser Hanger

We all have the problem, after having ever so carefully got a razor-sharp crease in our trousers, of preserving the crease whilst trying to get them evenly over the bar of the hanger. This contraption allows you to open the hanger and just place the breeches over the bar without any effort—and with a lot less nervous tension!

Goffering Iron for Ruffs

Looking like something out of a Victorian chemistry set, this was the answer to the problem of shaping all manner of cloth and linen. The tube was heated by inserting a metal poker-like rod fresh from a stove or hearth, then frilled cuffs and collars could be curled round the cylinder, whilst other trimmings, like ribbons, could be shaped upon it. While one is being used the spare poker is being heated.

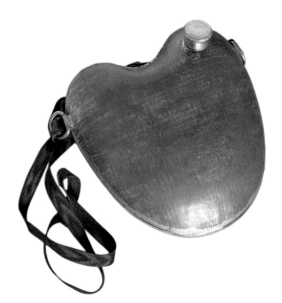

Warm Hearted

Heart-Shaped Hot Water Bottle

Made of metal and as big as one's hand, this heart-shaped heater would have been used under one's coat to keep warm whilst out in bad Victorian winters—a gift for Valentine's Day? Certainly a fond way of keeping your loved one snug and cherished.

Potable Water

In many parts of the world, lack of clean drinking water is still a major problem. Back in Victorian Britain it was a real threat to public health. Henry Doulton invented the modern ceramic sanitary water filter in 1827. In 1835, Queen Victoria commissioned him to produce such a device for her personal use, and by 1846, Doulton was widely recognized as the premier manufacturer of water filters, all by Royal appointment.

Doulton Filter

Just to comment on the beauty of this piece of pottery, irrespective of its functionality: it is wonderful to the touch. Charcoal would be inside the bowl and the water would gently trickle through.

Moveable Block Filter

Silicated carbon adsorbed more of the impurities from water than did charcoal filters alone. This portable block was ideal for those abroad or on expeditions.

Under Lock and Key

Hinged Key and Opener

As can be seen, the key is hinged and when bent becomes locked. The reason is that it also acts as a doorknob. You unlock the door, then, using the same hand, pull as you would the knob—clever those Victorians.

Police Key Tag

At the beginning of the twentieth century, it was common practice for your key chain to have a printed tag with a number attached. The idea was each key would be registered with the police. Your number is recorded against your name, so when the key is found, if handed back, it could be returned to the rightful owner.

If You Can't Stick Flies

Fly Puffer

The clever packaging makes this a neat invention. It doubles as a puffer, as well as being the container of the powder to get rid of a range of small insects. From the 1930s.

Fly Paper

Still in use today in some farmhouses, it wasn't that many years ago when fly papers were in common use to catch the little critters by attracting them with a strong aroma and then adhering them to a sticky surface. This example is from the 1920s.

Honing the Blades

The knife and scissor grinder was one of the street merchants whose call was most welcome in Victorian homes. He only came two or three times a year, but the warmth that greeted him was a result of the blades of the time not being made of stainless steel. As a result, they became blunt quickly and needed regular sharpening to keep their edge.

Scissor Sharpeners

Larger houses in Victorian and Edwardian times had their own blade sharpeners. Here are two examples: a permanent one to be kept in the kitchen and a portable scissor sharpener.

Changeable Scissor Blades

Even by the 1930s, scissor steel was still not as hard and durable as today. One answer to the problem of blunt blades was to have a spare sharp pair until the grinder could be used.

Knife Cleaner

It's the leather cover on the wheel that cleans the knives. Once again, the advertisement is aimed at the householder purchasing it for the servant. Produced in the late nineteenth century.

Fluting the Pleat

A wide variety of fluting irons (fluters) were manufactured in Victorian times; these examples are "rocker" style. All were improvements over the earlier method of pressing pleats into fabric that involved wrapping each individual crease by hand around a goffering iron. Ladies' and children's clothing of the late nineteenth century featured a lot of pleated (fluted or plaited) trim. These intricate ruffles and ruches created the need for the development of these new fluting irons.

Both these examples use a hand-operated corrugated roller; the fabric goes between the roller and the corrugations of the base to produce the crimping effect. The second device is a little more sophisticated, as the base lifts to reveal a cast iron base that can be heated with an iron. The heat makes the pleating easier and crisper. Yet to do an entire dress, especially the voluminous dresses of the mid-Victorian period, would have taken many exacting and laborious hours of manpower—almost certainly womanpower. Automation and efficiency were still some way off in this area.

Stop Thief

Burglar Traps

Truly alarming! The firework manufacturers must have created this little gadget to fill time when bangers were out of season. It seems to be able to fit any door. When opened the string is pulled and a loud bang is heard. Probably dates from the late 1940s.

Lock with Alarm

A clever idea from the days of clockwork. Integrated into this door lock is a simple clockwork alarm; if the wrong key is fitted off goes the alarm, making a horrendous racket. Just don't come in late and inebriated and accidentally choose the wrong key!

Hat and Clothes Lock

Used in London gentlemen's clubs, this would assure the member his items would still be there when he left the building and not have been filched by some cad, or by a fellow gentleman the worse for wear.

The Door Holder

Door Wedge

One of the niftiest ideas in the collection from the 1920s. The two rubberised ends are connected by thin, flexible metal. Bending the two ends allows it to slide easily under the door. The rubber ends grip the floor and hold the door firmly ajar, yet not so firmly as to prevent you adjusting the door's position. Even better, it acts as a door wedge in both directions at once. Brilliant!

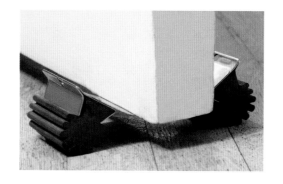

"Put That Light Out!"

Fly Catching Bulb

Such a great idea and oh so simple. All you had to do was put a little honey or jam into the aperture in the middle of the bulb, turn on the light, and wait. The pesky insect would be attracted by the light, be doubly attracted by the sweet smelling jam, and would get stuck in there, only to be incinerated by the heat of the lamp.

Blitz Blackout Bulbs

"Put that light out" was a catch phrase during the blitz in WWII. The use of a black bulb that gave just a glimmer resolved most of that problem, though no doubt not entirely to the satisfaction of Warden Hodges.

Broken Bulb Remover

The glass in Edwardian times was not of the same quality as today and bulbs often broke. This handy gadget allowed the nasty, jagged remains to be unscrewed safely from the bulb holder.

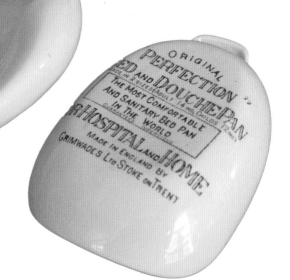

A Well-Aired Bed

Grimwade's Bed Pan, Salesman's Sample

Not in fact "perfection," but more of one of life's grim necessities.

Victorian Brick Warmer

It would have stood on a range or be placed in a fire to heat up, then used in the bed to keep you snug and warm.

Damp Sheet Tester

How would you have felt to be handed a damp sheet tester upon arrival at a hotel or guest house in the 1920s? The idea is you could use this hygrometer to prove the sheets were properly aired and dried—but what if they were not? "Excuse me, Mr. Fawlty, but my bedsheets are damp and not thoroughly aired . . . Mr. Fawlty?"

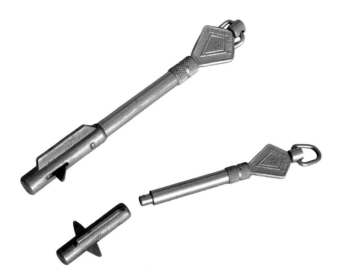

The Home As a Castle

Keyhole Protector

A very clever invention: in the early twentieth century, the occupant of a hotel room, upon leaving, would insert this apparatus, turn it, and then remove the key end, leaving inside the metal capsule that would prevent anyone else inserting a key. Only snag was, you then had two things you could lose: the key and the keyhole protector!

Clockwork Door Handle

The genius who thought up this little gadget was onto something really good. Here the alarm is set in the bulbous end, which, after setting by winding up, will go off if any attempt is made to turn the handle. So clever it really should have become a great success, but, sadly, there is no evidence the inventor made any money at all from this gadget.

Clockwork Alarm

Household security was just as big a challenge then as it is now. Edwardian inventors excelled when it came to defending the home from intruders. With electrical devices being expensive and electric motors and relays still quite cumbersome, clockwork was the main mode of operation. Here you have one of many below-the-door alarms. This one is not a wedge. Instead, fierce prongs underneath secure it to the carpet. If the door is pushed, the spike on the end sets off a very loud alarm to awaken the whole house. But that of course leaves the householder with an age old dilemma: whether to go downstairs and attempt to tackle the intruder, or whether, more prudently, to hope the alarm frightens him off.

In Case of a Pong

Hiding unpleasant aromas was just as much big business in the past as it is today.

Fragrant Pastilles

By setting light to this Edwardian pastille a healthy but strong aroma is emitted. More fumigator than air freshener!

Perfume Distributor

As you can see by the box top, the young Victorian lady is blowing the droplets of perfume through a pipette. It is hoped the obnoxious smells were only found in the "smallest room" and not everywhere in the house, as otherwise the poor lady may have expired either through inhalation of the scent or overexertion of the lungs before the whole house was "decontaminated!"

Disinfector

A much more complex machine that boils a mixture using the heater in the base. The perfumed vapour then escapes through the nozzle in the top. A forerunner of today's plug-in air fresheners.

Beating a Path!

The saying goes if you could produce a better mousetrap people would "beat a path to your door." Well, what do you think? Would you beat a path to these inventors' doors?

Glass Mousetrap

Dating from 1918.

Mouse Proof Pedal

We believe this was used on a church organ pedal. Pulling out the all the stops, so to speak, to prevent the little critters from gnawing away wooden foot pedals!

Mouse Trap 1930s

From the mouse's point of view the proverbial "jaws of Hell," and from the human point of view—would you be battering on the door?

Double-barelled Mousetrap

One for Minnie and one for Mickey?

Getting the Fly by Any Means

Fly Paper Plate

Throughout the ages, human beings have wanted to swat away flies to prevent the spread of disease. For all that time, creative thinkers have endeavoured to find ways of getting rid of the little critters. Here are just a few of the attempts, from the Fly-Paper Plate—just remember not to eat off it —to the wonderfully inventive Automatic Gun Swat, a boon to young boys everywhere!

Catch "More Than One" Swat

That's if you're quick enough!

Spring Swat

Looks like a "squash 'em flat" device!

Automatic Gun Swat

Alarmed!

Automatic Boot Remover

Place one foot into the claw, the other on the pedal, and one press and a pull and your foot is free. Dated 1900.

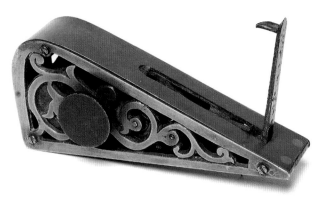

Clockwork Burglar Alarm

An ornate version of the door wedge alarm from 1880. If an intruder tried to open the door the lever went down, releasing a catch and setting off a very loud bell.

Roll-Over Burglar Alarm

Automatic Burglar Alarm

Yet another variation on the clockwork burglar alarm. In some ways one of the more ridiculous products of its type, but with three interesting features: it looks good, it is highly sensitive, and it is the precursor of electronic tilt switches. It really is sensitive on those three tiny legs—how often would it be set off by a cat giving it a bat with its paw, I wonder?

Door Alarm

A later variation on the clockwork door alarm from the late 1930s. If the door was opened and the plunger released it made plenty of racket to raise the whole household. Simple but effective.

Room for Ablutions

Whistling Snow White

Merchandising was alive and well in the late 1930s, as can be seen by this whistling toothbrush promoting the Disney film *Snow White*.

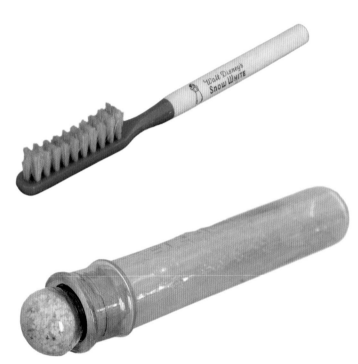

Toothbrush Steriliser and Container

The chemicals in the lid kept the brush free of germs.

Towel Clip

This elegant sprung towel holder was aimed at the upmarket home. As always, the Victorian manufacturer made sure the name of the device was displayed prominently, encouraging further sales to admiring visitors.

Potty Chimneys

Sail Chimney Cowling

By attaching a simple solid sail to the cowling and allowing it to rotate the smoke always blew with the wind. This example is late Victorian.

XIV.— That all Persons allowing their Chimney-vents to get dirty, and thereby to take fire, so as to incur the risk of damage to themselves, and neighbours, shall be subject to a penalty of Five Shillings, unless they are able to instruct, that the vent has been swept within Six Weeks preceding.

XV.— That all Ruinous Chimneys, or other buildings, shall be repaired by the proprietors, so as not to endanger the inhabitants; and any proprietor, after being required by orders from the Dean of Guild, to repair the same, failing so to do, within a given time, shall be subject to a penalty of Ten Shillings and Sixpence.

XVI.— That no persons, not being lawful owners, or occupiers of property, shall put Horses, or other Bestial out to pasture in the night-time, without the leave of some such owner or occupier; and no person shall put any Horses, or other Bestial out to pasture either by night or day on the open and unenclosed lands within the Burgh-roads, without either properly herding or tethering the same, —all under the penalty of Two Shillings and Sixpence, besides the Lawful POIND, and damages to those on whose property they may trespass, and all expences.

XVII.— That no persons shall fire Guns, Pistols, or other Fire arms on or near to the Streets, Lanes, Closes, or Roads, or in any Garden, Stackyard, or other place within the Burgh, or within the Burgh-roads, unless for the destroying of birds &c. in the necessary protection of their property, and in this case they shall not entrust the doing this to Boys, or Persons who may not proceed with proper Caution, under the penalty of Two Shillings and Sixpence, or Imprisonment, as shall be awarded by the Magistrates.

XVIII.— That any person failing to pay the above fines, on an order by the Magistrates, shall, over and above, be liable in the expence of any prosecution, which may be raised for the recovery thereof.

The MAGISTRATES appoint these BYE-LAWS, and REGULATIONS to be printed, and posted in the most public places of the Town, that none may pretend Ignorance thereof; and the Dean of Guild, Procurator Fiscal, Burgh Officers, and Constables, are specially charged to see that the same be strictly observed.

Selkirk

The Royal Burgh of Selkirk issued this notice to inhabitants in 1820; it lists all the fines that can be imposed on town folk if they don't obey the issued regulations. Points 14 and 15 indicate how they must keep their cowling clean—if not they would be fined five shillings—and how they had to keep their chimney in good repair.

Fireplace Stand or Trivet

Adjustable Trivet

Imagine the Victorian fireplace: roaring logs and red hot coals with the kettle alongside, just ready to be placed onto the flames. The kettle is stood on this lovely trivet hooked into the grill of the fireplace.

This stand is clearly not for the workaday kitchen; it could hold kettles or saucepans on fires in living rooms. The ceramic handle allows positioning as needed, either to hold a larger pan or to keep a dish warm at just the right distance from the heat of the fire.

THE ART OF SELLING

Modern marketing! Ah, for the good old days, when one was left in peace to select goods and services you really wanted without having brand names thrust in front of one at every opportunity. Don't you believe it!

A look at any old photograph of the average Victorian station or High Street will demonstrate how every available space was used to advertise wares; not an inch of space was wasted. Especially when there were so many manufacturers, lots of independent shops, and scores of banks and providers of services—getting one's name across was all important.

So was born the advertising agency. Soon the banners and the slogans, the clever imagery, and the strap-lines were in place. Modern marketing began long before WWI, as, too, did the trade show and all the promotional literature and stunts that went with them. As new technologies became available, just as in our own time with the Internet and social media, so advertising men and women moved in to attract our attention. No opportunity was lost.

Most interesting of all was the rise of the novelty give-away and the promotional gimmick. These probably had their heyday between the wars. Some of these are wonderfully inventive and fun—which is your favourite?

The Whirleygig

The problem of selling your wares was just as much a problem in the time of Queen Victoria as it is today. Now we have giant billboards on flat-bed trucks, with both sides promoting a product or service. Back in 1840, there was an even better system, the "Whirligig." As the horse draws the cart the advertising turns, showing all sides to pedestrians as it passes by.

Advertising Your Wares

The invention of products in the Victorian era was manifold. Tens of thousands of patents were lodged each year by inventors hoping to make their fortune in the burgeoning consumer market of the late nineteenth century. In the USA in particular, labour-saving gadgets were all the rage. But how to get yourself noticed in such a crowded marketplace?

These three flyers show the early development of advertising, from old-style handbills through detailed argument still to be found today amongst the franchise opportunities in newspapers, to bolder typefaces and generally less text.

The folding bath flyer was to find distributors for a new start up business. I have often wondered if it succeeded, or did the bottom fall out of the folding bath market?

Trade Shows

This flyer from 1889 illustrates a fundamental difference in the way exhibition space was sold when compared to the present day. As can be seen, you bought your space by the foot run, not the square foot. The Victorian organisers had cottoned onto the fact that it was aisle space you were buying, thus increasing your exposure to passing buyers.

Following 1851 and the Great Exhibition, this system of trade shows selling to specific markets developed rapidly and today there are thousands of trade shows world-wide, stimulating the world economy and keeping thousands of people employed.

Shop Till You Drop

Do you do your banking by phone, your shopping online, or do you download apps? Here is shopping by phone, 1910-style. The leaflet on the right is for the latest technology, the telephone! Harrods, Britain's number one store, has installed the very latest equipment for sales and what a wonderful number, "Western One." A very limited service, you may think. But no! How many customer phone lines today offer 24-hour service? In 1910, the Harrod's line was open day and night, and it would be answered by a real person, not the robotic voice we hear today offering a variety of choices. Even better, there would be no hanging on the line whilst being assured "Your call is very important to us."

The equivalent of online shopping from Victorian times up to the late twentieth century was the mail order catalogue. It started due to the remoteness of rural farming communities, especially in North America, but grew into a major industry. Stores like Harrods and Army and Navy produced annual catalogues of thousands of pages distributed by post world-wide, and what a godsend these old catalogues are to collectors like myself, because they help identify and date artefacts and even give the original sale price.

The Victorians loved posters, and by the Edwardian period, it seemed every square inch was plastered with posters: at railway stations, on billboards, hoardings, at football grounds, on the sides of buses, and shop fronts.

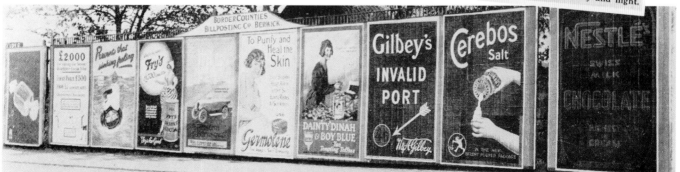

It's All at the Co-Op!

For over a century, the co-op was to be found on nearly every British High Street. The modern co-operative movement grew out of the friendly societies of the eighteenth and early nineteenth century. The principal was any profits from the business would be distributed back to all its members in the form of a dividend—the famous "divvy."

Earlier co-operatives tended not to have their own stores, but in 1844, the Rochdale Pioneers set up a proper business as a shop, selling good quality groceries, provisions, and hardware to working class families in town.

By the end of the nineteenth century, nearly every town in the UK had at least one co-operative store. Often there were several co-op buildings in one town, with grocers, butchers, bakers, haberdashers, drapers, milliners, chemists, furniture stores, hardware stores, and even funeral directors.

This lovely tea tray from 1922 is celebrating fifty years of the Cinder Hill Working Men's Co-operative Society in Basford, on the outskirts of Nottingham.

Advertising Coming of Age

By the 1930s, advertising was recognisably "modern," using attractive images, strong visuals, and even links to charities to increase interest.

Oh, for a Stove Like This!

Stove and Heater

Beautifully printed, this flyer warms on the outside by depicting the heating abilities of this stove and tickles your tastebuds on the inside by displaying its cooking and baking features.

"If Only We Had a Gramophone."

Gramophone sales card

Aspirational advertising: even in the rural Midwest folks could be encouraged to want a Zon-o-Phone. Opening the card just made you want one all the more.

Changing Faces

These advertising flyers were a simple way of getting over a sales message by having a card folded down the centre.

One part always remains the same. In these flyers, the top part of the face, usually showing the user sad, changes into a smiling face once the card is fully opened.

This demonstrates an interesting way of stopping children making holes in their breeches by using elasticised knee pads.

The Peep-o'-Day alarm clock is being praised in poetry by the man who, being so concerned he would not wake up for an appointment, would stay up all night until he purchased the alarm clock!

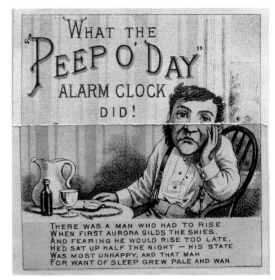

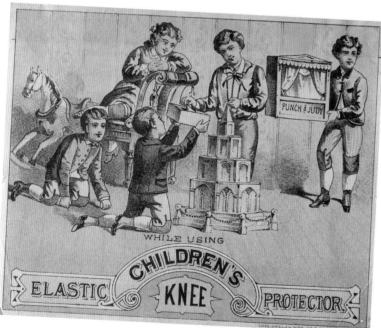

Knee Protector Card

Alarm Clock Card

Marking the Page

Bookmarks used to advertise products have been around from the late eighteenth century. It's a great idea for the reader to be reminded of your brand name at every turn of the page.

Port Bookmark

A very simple idea using celluloid that works very effectively. From around the 1930s. Complete with original bag and instructions.

Engineering a Sale with These Flyers

Long before electronic gizmos, simple cardboard mechanisms were in use to attract attention and win those all-important sales.

Rising Golfer

By simple cardboard engineering this card, when opened, shows the golfer rising, ready to hit the ball. The card is dated 1910, complete with testimony.

Pears' Soap Bookmarks

Beautifully designed with the simple mechanism of a slit around the fingers pointing to the page at which you left off reading. Late nineteenth century.

Brushing Teeth

This cardboard cut-out shows a young girl cleaning her teeth. The brush rises to her mouth as you open the card. It is selling fruit-flavoured Colgate toothpaste for children, around 1930.

Printers' Stock Flyers

These cut-out advertising cards would be printed on the reverse with any sales message a customer requested. Similar to the formats for printing flyers and cards on computers today.

Digging for Lids

Advertising Pot Lids

It was Felix Edward Pratt (1813–94) who noticed the possibilities of using new printing technology to decorate lids of containers for popular products, such as bear's grease, gentleman's relish, potted shrimps, toothpaste, and ointments and cosmetics with hard selling designs.

After 1840, his firm, F. & R. Pratt of Fenton in Staffordshire, became the leading but not the only manufacturer of multicoloured transfer printed pot lids and a huge range of related wares.

The lids in the collection come from bottle digs; that is, finding Victorian rubbish dumps and digging down till you reach the layers of rubbish put there in the late nineteenth century, where you can find bottles, clay pipes, and these advertising pot lids.

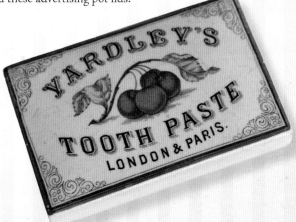

Not a Chance Missed

Even more than today, Victorian and Edwardian advertisers used every opportunity to get their message across. A good example is a typewriter advert on the back of a ladies' hand mirror; just the thing for the Edwardian office. The other two examples are both promotional pincushions—again aimed at women—with two very different products. The top one is for boots from the Walk-Over Shoe Company—someone must have had a lot of fun coming up with that name. The second one is a bit of a curiosity; advertising an early centrifugal water cooler on the back of a pincushion sounds like a nice idea, but including Grease Catch Basins rather lowers the tone!

Shadow Advertising

Ah, those simple days! There is something quite delightful and also slightly perversely eerie about this novel form of advertising; the baby looks just too upset at big sister pinching Mellin's soft drink.

But what an inventive idea, even if it is the "Shadow of a Crime!"

Guess What the Oracle Says!

You have a nasty cold, a sudden chill, influenza, a splitting headache, chronic rheumatism, or a touch of the vapours. Who do you turn to for help? You ask the oracle of course. This give-away from Beecham's now sounds only like a fire hazard, but novelty in advertising was everything.

So what answer does the Oracle give to ease your pain? Well, when you light the touch paper, the burning reveals —surprise, surprise—the word "BEECHAMS." Dated around the 1930s.

Selling Pastimes

Boots, the well known British chain of chemists, launched a major advertising campaign in 1935 around the slogan "See How They Won." It was genuinely multi-media, with a short advertising film for the cinema, a record released, newspaper advertisements, and this colourful promotional board game.

Game of Good Health - Boots

The board game is a classic roll-the-dice game where the products are part of every move. For example: "When you have a cold, take an aspirin." At every throw of the dice Boots had the answer!

Dominoes by Nestlé's

Another marketing give-away. Not only is the game branded by the chocolate maker, but every domino reminds you of their condensed milk products: "Richest in Cream."

Advertising Spinning Fan

Even in Edwardian times advertisers never missed a trick. Here a baby food manufacturer came up with an amazing spinning fan. It may even have been intended to keep little George or Georgina cool in the cot. Plasmon is still going as Italy's leading baby and nutritional supplement brand, though owned by a well known American firm with more than fifty-seven varieties.

Not only is the gadget so well designed, but the advertisement is full of colour, using the same "puffery" as in today's copywriting.

Spinning Fan

You turn the shaped advert until the elastic is totally wound up, then release and it turns at a reasonable rate to give some fresh cool air to the user. Simple yet effective.

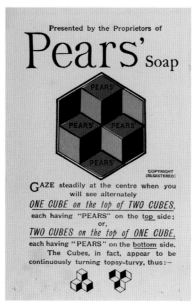

"Brain Washing!"

Brand Image

You've got to hand it to them, these are outstanding advertising stunts. Long before the Internet and social media, campaigns latched on to novelty to get the brand name across. There is nothing here about how efficacious Pear's Soap can be; instead, it is all about imprinting the brand name on the minds of the curious.

Yet compared to the fleeting attention span of the present-day consumer, Pear's expected you to concentrate for a whole minute! In that time the name Pear's would not only be seared onto your retina, but would be lodged in your brain forever. Brilliant!

Getting Your Voice Heard!

Record Postcards

Pre-recorded music could be sent to those that had gramophones back in the '20s. Radio was beginning to take hold, but for a short period this was the latest way of sending music cheaply. A bit like sharing the playlist from your iPod™.

Advertising by Record

Junk mail is not new! Here is the thirties equivalent of spam, Internet advertising, or following us on Facebook®. The recorded message was carefully targeted at particular consumers, so nothing new there, then.

I wonder how many ever found their way on to the gramophone, especially as you had to fiddle with the wooden needles?

"Crikey!" Shell Speaks for Itself

Shell Talking Advertisement

From the 1930s and part of a major and well known Shell campaign ("You can be sure of Shell"), this very rare talking advertisement is based on the idea their petrol is quick starting: the car is here and then it is off in a flash. I am unsure of the mechanics of this talking advert, but here's how it works: Hold the talking box in your right hand with the label facing you and the short end of tape in your left hand. Pull the box steadily away from left to right and you will hear "Crikey! - That's Shell - That was!" Perhaps it was just too difficult to get it to say, "You can be sure of Shell!"

The sales agent is in London, but the product was manufactured in the States.

Yours for Free

Advertising Projector

By the 1920s they were all at it. This was the start of the height of promotional give-aways. Here are three interesting examples.

The one for the Co-operative Society doesn't mess around with fancy typefaces and the result is a piece of naïve advertising artwork. As you tilt the card, the lady on the phone winks—all for a cream cracker!

Next we have a needle threader promoting a brand of vanilla essence and a set square given away by Lifebuoy soap—for your health.

Don't Look under the Plate!

Advertising Plate

Their four-month-old "Teddy Bear" may ruffle modern sensibilities, but the sheer audacity of this advertising plate from Thomas Wallis of London is quite stunning. The rather immature advertising ploy to implore people not to look under the plate may have been a trifle gauche, but it worked, and just look at the amazing range of goods on offer!

FLAMING LIGHTS

Put that light out! The Victorians were caught between not having enough heat and light and having far too much. Period dramas on television nowadays are often criticised for being too authentic. It is often difficult to make out in the drab, dark light what is going on. A single candle flame may have been all the Victorian householder had to illuminate their house, but it doesn't make for easy television viewing.

Even when oil lamps and early gas mantles became common, most interiors were dark, sooty affairs. Not only did the Victorian household struggle in the half-light, but they had a devil of a job staying warm. Coal fires had to be kept banked up, and, if they did not draw well, might only add to the smoke and soot inside the house.

The Victorians wanted more light and flame, but, like generations before, they also wanted less. The danger of an unattended candle or a spark causing a fire was very great. People were quite often burned in their beds. The wonderful array of "Go to Beds" in this collection needs to be put alongside the early attempts at fire extinguishers.

In this section are an array of inventive gadgets from a time when light and heat were indeed matters of life and death.

Eyes for the Bedroom

Go to Bed

This charming ceramic light was carried upstairs, though it lacks a handle. Under the bell-like dome cover are small, thin wax candles. Each would last only a few minutes—just long enough to get into your nightshirt and under the covers on a cold winter's night in the days long before central heating.

Common Go to Bed

In its simplest form, the apparatus is just a circular container with waxed matches inside and a striker at its base, but it still has some adornment.

Go to Bed Set

This lovely brass go to bed has all the paraphernalia needed to maintain light in its best working condition. The snips, in a neat aperture at the base of the stick, are ready to sharpen the wick, and the conical snuffer would put out the flame.

Holding a Torch

The streets of most Victorian towns and cities were in darkness at night, with only main roads lit by gaslight. The foot traveller needed some means to light the way and to provide at least a semblance of security and these "candle torches" were the answer at the time.

Book Torch

This book torch is particularly novel, having a container for an extra candle in its "spine" and a match compartment and striker.

Folding Lantern

This torch had similar compartments and, like the book torch, folded down flat to be easily carried in one's pocket. One snag: the transparent film through which the light projects is a mica paper, making it very flimsy and easily torn.

Spills and SOS

Lifeboat Matches

Produced in the 1930s in a watertight plastic box with striking sides, Bryant and May made these long lasting lights specifically to be stored in lifeboats on ships so that, should the worst happen, they could give a little light at night and act as a small flare to help locate stranded at sea.

Plastic Spill Dispenser

Board Spill Dispenser

Paper spills were cut from these dispensers and then twisted to make them stronger. They were then used to light cigarettes or stoves from open fires. Given how cheap matches were even then, whether you could actually save money by buying paper spills is debateable.

At the Hearth

Chestnut Roaster

With a lovely cockerel design on the pan, this Victorian roaster would be placed on the embers with chestnuts inside. It has a neat mechanical lift mechanism to check on the progress of the nuts. Makes you want to curl up in front of the fire!

Toasting Fork

A toasting fork with a difference: you can swivel the head so you can get the bread face on to the glowing embers from any angle. Scrumptious!

Clockwork Fire Blower

A surprising use for good old clockwork. You wind up the spring to give energy, then attach it to the metal bars of the fire grate. Then you release the spring, which turns the bellows, causing air to fan the fire's embers—instead of putting paper in front of the fire—remember those days?

Striking a Light

Flintlock Tinder Pistol

To ignite gunpowder, a flintlock pistol produced a spark when a piece of flint sprang against steel, so why not use it to produce a flame that could ignite a fire in a grate, light a stove, or get a bonfire going? Inevitably Tinder Pistols were expensive and owned only by a small and wealthy minority of households. They were often converted by a gunsmith from ordinary pistols. This model is from around 1830. It is a beautifully crafted firearm with wooden handle, steel trigger and hammer head, brass body, tinder well, and cabriole-leg-shaped rest.

Go to Bed

Lady with Basket Go to Bed

There was the Go to Bed candle, which got you up to your room, and then there were these Go-to-Bed or Getting-into-Bed matchboxes.

Relatively small (about 6 cm high), they were frequently made of metal of some kind, though sometimes of wood or ivory. Most incorporated a rough surface on which the match could be struck. All featured a small hole or finial, sometimes in ivory and always part of the design, into which the lighted match could be placed, rather like a miniature candle. The idea was, rather than risk taking a lighted candle near bed, the lighted match on the mantelpiece would burn for some thirty seconds—just long enough for the person to snuff out the candle and hop into bed.

Once a necessity, they now appear as attractive curios.

Barrel Go to Bed

Hand Go to Bed

The Burglar's Horror

Candle Adhesive

As described on the lid, one drop on the base of a candle the size of a pea holds the candle in place.

Candle Clip and Holder

Fitting with a jaw-like grip, this holder keeps the candle held firmly upright and could be adjusted to different diameter candles. The risk of fire starting from a candle flame was a terrifying prospect throughout Victorian times.

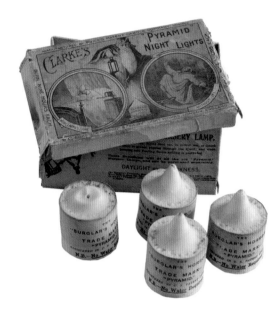

Pyramid Night Lights

Clarke's promoted their candles as being a security device. Here you have every wax light branded "The Burglar's Horror." Not sure as to their efficacy—they are only candles after all.

Atlas Candle Grip

A seriously well engineered device to keep a firm grip on candles and thus help prevent fires. Note it contains "No Soldered Parts" and that "All Parts are Rivetted and Screwed." Possibly a sledgehammer to crack a nut, but a further example of the robustness of invention.

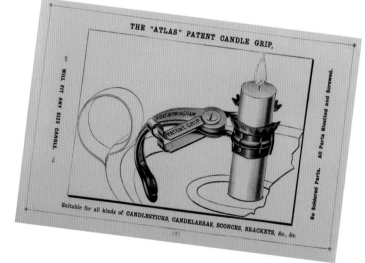

Setting the World Alight

Fire Blower

Another lovely example of how, for the wealthy at least, invention was made attractive. Rather than being moved from room to room, these beautifully crafted blowers would be on every hearth in a large nineteenth century mansion. Just ring the bell, and the housemaid would come running to wind the wheel and encourage a sluggish fire to burst into life. Of course the aim had to be right, but even that could be adjusted.

Ceramic Coal Ball

Looking like a lesser known moon of the planet Jupiter, this ball was lodged amid the coals to help air get to all parts of the fire. Must have been a difficult job to clean it of all the ash inside it the next morning—yet another job for the maid.

Fire Grenade

Take aim! If a fire started you could lob this glass ball at the conflagration to put out the flames. Early examples such as this from 1850 onwards contained a strong solution of bicarbonate of soda, but later ones used carbon tetrachloride, which would put out a fire but was also highly poisonous.

Candle Power

Floating Candles

Putting these candles in a bowl of water you have a mass of light that gives a wonderful effect.

Night Light

Mechanical Candle Snuffer

One of the more amazing candle inventions, the automatic snuffer. Placed over a candle, the two top sprung lips close and snuff the candle. Victoria's coat of arms is on the side. Would Her Majesty have been amused by this apparently over-elaborate device?

Gadgets for Candles

Bottle Candle Holder

A clever patent to allow empty bottles to be used as candle sticks. It has a cork to fit in the wine bottle and a rim so no candle wax runs down the sides of the bottle in the manner so beloved of TV period dramas and certain types of restaurants.

Puffer Extinguisher

A mid-twentieth century attempt to mechanise the snuffing-out of candles. Children would love this one.

Candle Snuffer

A standard gadget in many homes; a quick clip of the wick puts out the light. Notice how even this most common of Victorian devices has been beautifully crafted, with natty little legs so it would sit flat on a dresser.

Fire! Blow the Whistle

The greatest change of the last 100 years has been from the mechanical to the electronic. Not having transistor switches to make decisions millions of times a second, the Victorian inventor had only solid "things" to use to determine whether a fire had started. Even so, there were workable mechanical devices and there were extraordinary early attempts at mechanising alarms, such as the one shown here.

Ballbearing Fire Alarm

This very unusual and early Victorian fire alarm is the most "Heath Robinson" concept I have come across. The clockwork alarm is wound up and the barrel is tipped forward and tied down with cord. As a result, a large ball bearing rolls to the far end. When a fire started it would burn through the cord, the barrel would tip back, and the ball would roll back along the barrel, trigger a switch, and the bell would ring.

Of course, by then it may well have been too late. A brave attempt, but heat sensitive mechanical alarms and automatic sprinklers were the answer.

Fire Whistle

We believe this was a whistle strapped on the wrist of sailors to warn the rest of the crew should a fire be spotted below deck.

Getting on One's Wick!

The Bell Soot Stopper

Hung from the ceiling, the glass bell shaped hood would stop any marks from burning candles underneath. From the late Victorian period.

Looks like a wizard idea, though mind when you clean it: all that soot and candle grease would make it very slippery and easy to let fall and break, and, if you were the servant, it might be your wages that would be docked.

Candle Sharpener

For sharpening the bottom end of candles, ensuring an easy and secure fit into the candlestick—a really useful safety device.

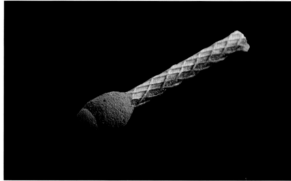

Strike a Light!

Cigar Match and Box

Specially made for lighting cigars.

Match Box Lock

We are unable to discover the purpose of this simple Edwardian lock. Perhaps to stop your matches being nicked? Or perhaps to keep them safe from children.

Victorian Go to Bed

There were many patents taken out on lighting your way to the bedroom by candlelight. They would often be like this "Go to Bed," with matches and small candles that fit into the lid of the container. The person then could put it down by the side of the bed as a nightlight if needed. Given how many died from fire, the whole thing was terribly dangerous, but with no electricity, and if you had no oil lamp, this at least showed you the way.

More Candle Power

Candle Snuffer

A typical snuffer that would be found in most Victorian middle class homes.

Bun Candle Holder

These holders all unscrew and then the two sides screw together in the shape of a "bun." It also contains a flame douser. They were made as travelling candle holders in the late nineteenth century.

Matchbox Candle Holder

A lovely illustrated matchbox that contains wax match candles. You strike the phosphorous and it burns away for several minutes. The real innovation here is to have a hole to place the candle in to light your way to bed. Simple and rather sweet.

Show Me the Way Home

Candle Torches

Without oil lamps and before gas lamps, these devices were the torches of their day. They were used to get about the house or to give at least a little light on one's way home at night. The one on the left is cheap and cheerful. The one on the right is both safer and more ornamental. I wonder how effective they were, and if the wind blew you would soon have no light at all. With pea-soup fogs, no wonder Victorians were so taken with ghost stories and Gothic tales.

Portable Self-Adjusting Candle Light

This delightful and ingenious candle lamp could be used as a torch or as a hanging light in the house. The innovation was the candle holder was sprung and telescopic; as the wax burnt down the spring pushed the candle up, ensuring the wick would always be in the right place. So just open the little doors and let the light shine out.

And So to Bed . . .

Bed Warmer and Airer

Produced in the 1920s, this was the latest technology for keeping a bed warmed and aired. Simply boil the ceramic element, pull up the central coil to disperse the heat, place in bed, and presto, nice and cosy!

The copywriter must have worked hard on the "S" message. But how odd to modern ears that the product was only "satisfactory." Today it would have to be superb, splendid, superior, super, superlative, stupendous, sensational, sublime, scintillating, and even splendiforous, but surely not merely satisfactory!

Bed-Linen Smoother

This wooden bat-like object would have been used by Victorian servants to smooth bed linen when making beds. Then you could always play softball cricket in the ballroom. Just mind the chandeliers!

Making the Necessary Beautiful

Ceramic Oil Lamp

Oil lamps have existed since ancient times. As well as providing at least a little light, they were also decorative and often had religious significance. The original materials used to make oil lamps included silver, gold, bronze, terracotta, and stone, with fired clay the most common.

Next came Argand lamps, which used whale oil. Then, in the 1850s, these were superceded by kerosene lamps. They, in their turn, were eventually made redundant by electricity.

Oil lamps are quite common and can easily be picked up in antique shops or on the Internet. However, a collection of gadgets would not be complete without one, and this example is particularly fine in decoration and effect.

WAR AND PEACE

No collection of gadgets, gizmos, and contraptions from the first half of the twentieth century can ignore the world wars and unstable peace. Though this collection is principally interested in the peaceful application of new technologies and social history, the dangers many faced cannot be ignored.

So, whilst this is not a collection devoted to militaria, here is a snapshot of nations at war. Gadgets are still here, especially ingenious portable household wares that came from earlier conflicts and expeditionary days.

Here, too, is a glimpse of life on the home front, from the gentle but persistent propaganda war to ARP wardens. The techniques of advertising agencies were put to full use, especially during WWII.

Most poignant of all are items like the full-suit baby gas mask. The potential fear of poison gas and the very real fear of air raids in Britain during those difficult years can be seen clearly. People fought and worked hard for victory even as they yearned for peace.

Collapsible Cup And Compass

Campaign Cup and Compass

The Edwardian adventurer or army officer would pull up on some dusty road and want to quench his thirst and take his bearings, and this ingenious gadget saw to both.

Campaign products of this sort were manufactured in large numbers. Compactness and lightness were essential, so they brought out the best in Edwardian designers.

This applied even to furniture, wash stands, toilets; in fact, anything that would have been needed in the field to ensure an efficient army or a successful expedition. Just the stuff for the upper reaches of the Congo or the northwest frontier.

You're in the Army Now

Army Blanco

If you have served in the army, you will appreciate just how important "Blanco" is to the average soldier, especially when doing your early training and for "square bashing." It is the pigment used to colour and clean equipment. This one, from Pickering's, is a standard khaki colour.

Forces Postal Records

In WWII, these postal records allowed men in North Africa or the Far East to record a message for their family back home—a precursor of email and text messages.

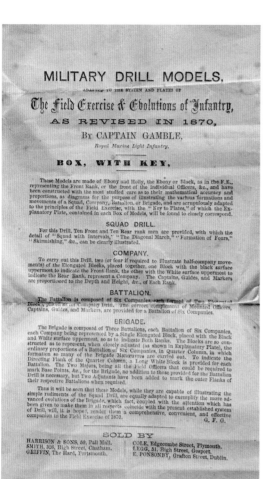

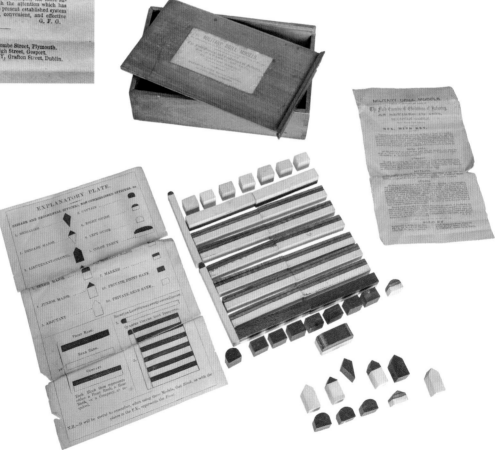

Right, You 'Orrible Lot!

War gaming for sergeant-majors, but no toy cannon fired a shot and no toy soldier was killed. This square bashing kit is complete with wooden blocks and bricks to represent every rank of officer, adjutants, cavalry, and the poor bloody infantry. Dating from 1870, the sergeant-major or the colonel could spend many happy hours planning the next drill parade, whether in Aldershot or in the heat of India.

Military Drill Models

Those who served in the armed forces and did daily drill will rarely have realised there was a formal layout "gadget" even for planning the order of the parade ground!

Each officer's rank had its wooden symbol, as did the "other ranks." The general could be in the comfort of his HQ, explaining to his subordinates how he wanted the parade ground set for his inspection!

Collapsible Candle Trench Lamp WWI

Fitting snugly into its own linen case, this could be easily assembled to bring light to the dugouts at the front.

Out on Campaign

Campaign or "knockdown" furniture, as it was often called, had its roots in the Napoleonic wars. The concept of easy to carry and easy to assemble items to assist officers at the front directed inventors to a flurry of activity—everything for the army life or a trek in the Himalayas.

Tent Pole Rifle Holder

Tent Pole Hanger

Pen Rack

Just a quick push on the sides allows this metal rack to collapse for easy carriage. Notice you can stack no fewer than nine pens—enough writing implements to pen *War and Peace*!

Collapsible Shaving Kit with Heater

No need to get in a lather as to how one will shave!

On the Front Line

Sniping Mirror

An invaluable addition to the rifle during the Great War, it is a miniature periscope which fits on the end of the rifle. It gives just that bit of extra height to let a poor Tommy decide whether it was wise to raise his head, take aim, and shoot.

Powder Flask

The clever patent in the head of this flask from the mid-Victorian period allowed you to set the amount of powder needed for different types of muzzle-loading guns. Too little and it would be a damp squib; too much and it might be a nasty shock, as well as still not firing the gun.

Cartridge Remover

When out on the moors, ready with your shotgun to down the pheasant, this little contraption allows you to remove the spent cartridge.

WWI Mechanical Cards

Mechanical Postcards

You can imagine that in WWI, with all the menfolk in the trenches in France, postcards had a massive boom. You could keep in touch every day with a card, but if you really wished to make your man laugh, cards that told a small tale would be sent. In truth, it's a little difficult to get the joke 100 years on.

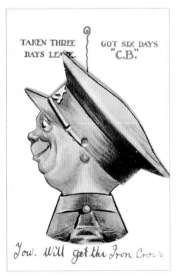

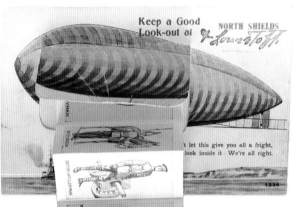

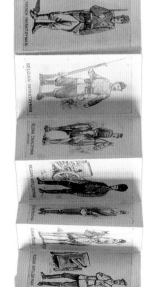

Drop-Out Card

A very common system of showing a range of different subjects would be the card that opened and out would fall tiny photographs. In this case it is pictures of different regiments fighting abroad. The phrase "keep a good look out" would be the sort of card that would be sent from the soldiers on the front line back to North Shields or wherever, though in this case the squaddie appears to have been from Lowestoft.

From the Parade Ground to the Trenches

WWI Kite Survival

Being a pilot in WWI was even more dangerous than being in the trenches. When aircrew were forced to bale out of their stricken aircraft they went with a parachute, an inflatable dinghy, and this possible life saver, a metal barrel containing a "kite." The idea was that if you did manage to inflate the dinghy and scramble aboard, the "kite" might act as a sail to help speed you back to the white cliffs of Dover and good old Blighty—as long as the wind was in the right direction!

WWI Siren Clackers

For most of the twentieth century, these extremely noisy wooden rattles were more likely seen at football matches, but during WWI they had a much more serious purpose: warning of a possible gas attack. These particular clackers work not by twirling but by pushing against the sides of a trench.

Pacing Stick

"I want you exactly 11 and 3/8 of an inch apart, you horrible lot!" When the sergeant major was lining up his troops on the parade ground, he made sure each soldier was exactly the same distance from the next by using this measuring stick. Fully adjustable, it left nothing to chance.

Trench Periscope

Looking rather dapper now, this piece of kit was essential in the trenches. It was quite dangerous enough without actually sticking your head above the parapet. These trench periscopes and larger versions were the answer

Eating Irons

Picnic Kit

Your knife, fork, and spoon, all available in a neat leather pouch. Just one handle and three attachments that click into place with a very smooth action. Not forgetting a corkscrew for the perfect picnic flourish!

Collapsible Spoon

Possibly from WWI, it fit neatly in the top pocket of a soldier's tunic, ready for any grub that might be on offer. The lever action mechanism allowing the gadget to collapse to half its size is an unusual design and very well engineered.

Knives, Pins, and Bullets

Scissors and Knife

This simple multi-tool's main purpose was as a pair of collapsible scissors, but they added the two knives. Possibly for the cigar smoker. From the 1920s.

Map Pins

Such a simple item from WWI. These would have been used by officers at the front to depict the deployment of their forces. To think that such an item needed to be patented.

WWII Prisioners' Work

Pen Knife

Not being able to identify the country of origin of the bullet, it's impossible to know if this piece of "trench work" came from the Allies or German forces, but it's a very neat piece of craftsmanship.

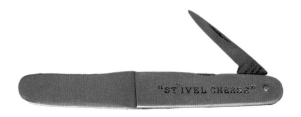

Cheese Knife

We all know St. Ivel cheese. This was a premium from the 1950s that kept their name in front of their customers, or at least in their pocket. An ideal pen knife for the working man and a cheese knife at the other end to spread the St. Ivel Lactic Cheese on a hunk of bread.

Patriotic WWII Teapot

When aluminium was needed in the war effort, even your good old bashed metal teapot was worth giving up. The enterprising mail order firm Dyson & Horsfall of Preston stepped in to the breach by having these souvenir china teapots made. Not only did they keep the cheering cuppas coming, but, covered with the flags of the initial Allies, they reflected the fighting spirit of all those working on the home front.

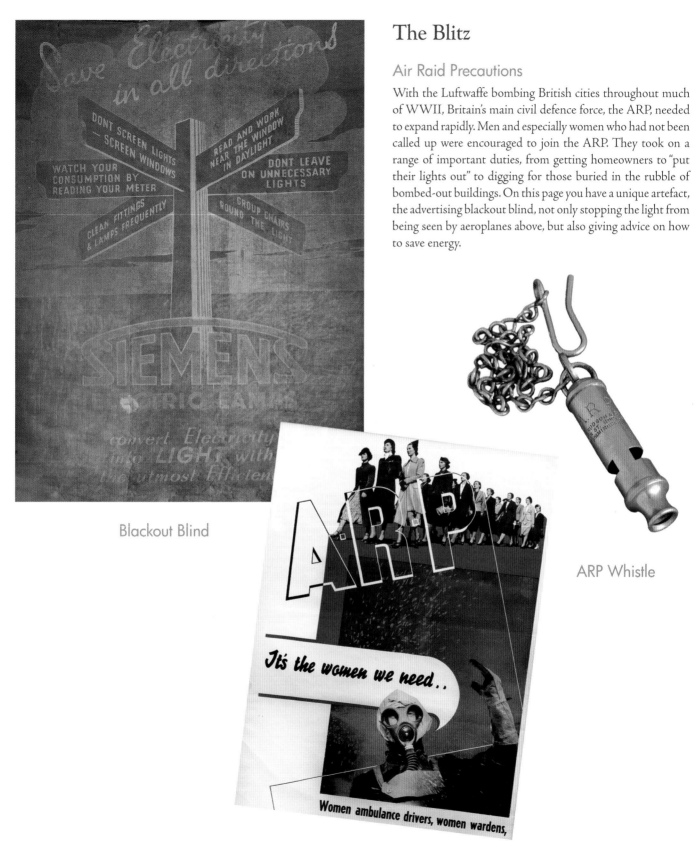

The Blitz

Air Raid Precautions

With the Luftwaffe bombing British cities throughout much of WWII, Britain's main civil defence force, the ARP, needed to expand rapidly. Men and especially women who had not been called up were encouraged to join the ARP. They took on a range of important duties, from getting homeowners to "put their lights out" to digging for those buried in the rubble of bombed-out buildings. On this page you have a unique artefact, the advertising blackout blind, not only stopping the light from being seen by aeroplanes above, but also giving advice on how to save energy.

Blackout Blind

ARP Whistle

Original Recruitment Poster

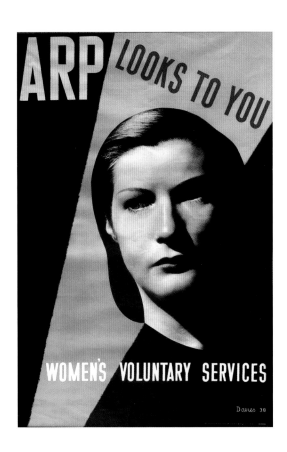

Air Raid Precautions

ARP

During WWII, the home front required a force to cope with the bombings that took place across the cities of Britain. This gas mask would be issued to all those brave men and women who were part of that elite civilian corps. The poster is a rare original copy encouraging women to become ARP wardens; it was mainly older men, such as Warden Hodges in *Dad's Army*, or those unfit for the forces who were at the heart of the service.

Don't Panic!
Platoon, Fix Roller Skates!
WWII - Home Guard

Army Issue Roller Skates

What if the Germans had got across the Channel? In 1940 it was touch and go, but by 1942, when these roller-skated boots were issued to Home Guard units, the Panzer divisions would have been up against a fully mobile *Dad's Army*. The picture in the box lid is genuine, not a still from the TV series. All the same, one can just imagine Capt. Mainwaring and Cpl. Jones roller skating along the front at Walmington-on-Sea between the pier and the Rock Emporium.

Babies' Gas Mask

There are frivolous items, but there are also those that are deadly serious. In 1938, the British government issued gas masks to the entire population, so serious was the threat taken that Germany might drop poison gas bombs at the start of the inevitable war. Some means to protect babies had to be developed.

This gas mask was for children up to two years old. The baby was placed inside the mask so the head was inside the helmet and the baby could see through the visor. Then the parents wrapped the canvas part around the baby's body with the straps fastened under its bottom, allowing its legs to dangle. The canvas had a rubber coating to stop gas seeping through, but the bottom was merely tied with cord.

There was an asbestos filter on the side of the mask to absorb poisonous gases. The baby breathed air pumped into the mask by a handle and bellows on the far side. Of course, this required the constant attention of the parent. Thankfully, despite all the death and destruction of the Blitz, this was one wartime kit that was never used in earnest.

The Great Escape

Helping prisoners of war escape was serious business during WWII; included are these undercover devices.

Escape Button Royal Air Force

Enclosed inside the button is a miniature compass to give downed aircrew a chance of finding their way to friendly territory. Sadly, if captured the Germans would be on to this straight away.

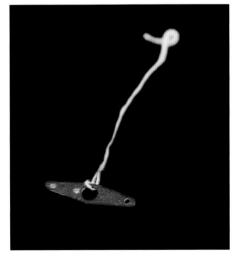

Magnetised Razor Blade

When floated on water (surface tension) the blade would swing to magnetic north.

Escape Collar Insert Compass Needle

This magnetised piece of metal would, when dangled on a piece of cotton, always point north.

Shirt Button Compass

As the Germans got wise to the button with the insignia normal shirt buttons did the job of direction, as long as you knew which hole was north.

Escape Saw

We don't believe this example is WWII, but later. It was used by British commando units.

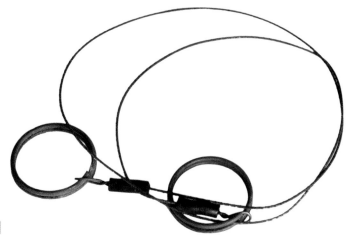

Escape Collar Stud

There were many escape gadgets provided to the RAF in WWII; this tiny item is a compass inside a collar stud. For those who are unaccustomed to detached collars, in the armed services your collar was separate from your shirt. You used a stud to fasten the collar to the shirt.

The bottom of the stud was covered in thick white cloth in an effort to go undetected by one's captors.

The Price of War

War has always produced new innovations and concepts, in the main to reap destruction on your enemy, but here we have items to aid soldiers, keep waste down, and house those severely wounded in time of war.

WWII Shoe Shine Mitt

Bulling one's boots in the army took an extraordinary amount of time. The boots had to shine to such an extent that you could see your reflection in the toe cap. The Americans made the job slightly easier by producing this aid to the shine, the gloved mitt. It is not entirely clear whether the glove itself contained any polish. Even if it did, the suggestion it would only take a minute to get a good shine was surely way wide of the mark!

Envelope Saver on the Home Front

Can you imagine the number of envelopes used in WWI? Millions of men at the front and the folks at home writing letters, some every day, to their loved ones. This very simple idea of using a single sheet of paper to overlay on the envelope conserved the use of paper and at the same time added to the funds of the British Sailors' Society—every little helps!

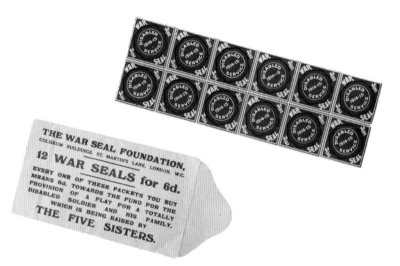

Housing Charity

Many men came out of the armed services seriously disabled in the Great War of 1914–1918. Here is one, simple charitable effort to help them. The money raised by selling these envelope "War Seals" went towards providing flats for injured servicemen.

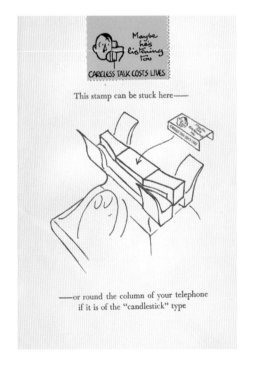

Careless Talk Costs Lives

The simplest ideas are often the most effective, never more so than in times of national emergency. During WWII, the British cartoonist Fougasse used his amazing graphic skills to create a range of propaganda posters and cartoons to help the war effort and to influence people to keep any secrets they might have. The possibility of enemy agents in our midst was very real.

He embarked on a series of cartoons with Hitler hidden in a range of different everyday scenes, such as sitting behind you on a bus, under the table in a restaurant, hiding behind a gatepost, or in a portrait on the wall in a gentleman's club listening to the chat. Thousands of these cartoons were printed and distributed throughout Britain.

Here is one of the smallest examples of Fougasse's work, and also one of the smallest "gadgets" in the collection, being just one inch by one inch. This little piece of blue gum paper was produced in 1940; the idea was to stick it onto the receiver handle of the telephone as a constant reminder that Hitler or his agents could be listening in, along with the succinct and very effective wartime slogan "CARELESS TALK COSTS LIVES."

Cyril Kenneth Bird, pen name Fougasse (December 17, 1887–June 11, 1965), was a British cartoonist best known as the editor of *Punch* magazine and for his WWII propaganda posters. He also designed many posters for the London Underground.

He was seriously injured at the Battle of Gallipoli during WWI and was invalided out of the British Army (his pen name is based on the fougasse, a type of mine). He first contributed to *Punch* in 1916, while convalescing, and also contributed to several other British newspapers and magazines, including the *Graphic* and the *Tatler*.

Foiling with Silhouettes

Window Strips

Some inventions are so simple yet so vital. This is just a coil of metal foil you might think, but it is a roll of the famous "window" foil, which when cut into pieces and dropped from RAF bombers confused German radar, thus concealing the whereabouts of Allied bombers.

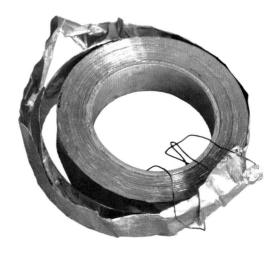

Aircraft Height Finder

During WWII, this booklet not only gave you the means to identify enemy aircraft, but also allowed you to work out the height of incoming planes—an invaluable tool for the Observer Corps.

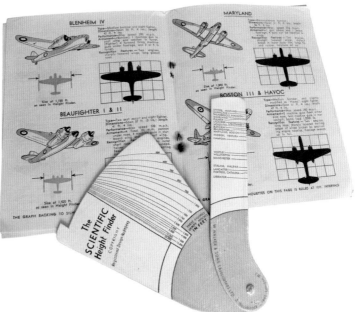

FOOD AND DRINK

A lot of the efforts of inventors in Victorian times went to mechanising food preparation, especially in the large kitchens of big houses. The section on Mechanising the Kitchen takes you on a tour of the scullery and "downstairs."

In this section you will find the smaller gadgets: the novel improvements for the table. Once again, most of these are intended for the country house, mansion, and town house with servants, for only those households could afford to go beyond the basics of cups, mugs, plates, bowls, and a spoon and knife.

Two of the most frequently met needs of the better-off householder appear to have been keeping the servants out of the brandy and keeping boiled eggs warm. The latter now seems slightly odd, but remember, this was in the days when the sumptuous Victorian breakfast was at its height, from devilled kidneys to lamb chops, from kippers to, yes, boiled eggs.

So enjoy perusing the inventiveness of the late-Victorian mind as you spread the marmalade thickly on the toast, take a sip of breakfast tea, fold your copy of the morning newspaper, and consider tackling the crossword in the time it takes to boil an egg!

Keeping Eggs Warm

Single Egg Warmer

This nifty table item would be filled with boiling water via the bottom screw. When the egg comes out of the pan it goes to the table with its own spoon ready for use.

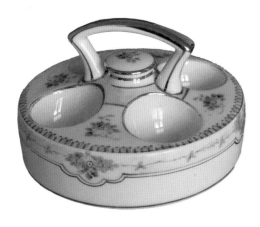

Four Egg Warmer

Filling this lovely Victorian ceramic dish with boiling water allowed the maid to serve to the table the eggs from the master's or mistress's kitchen piping hot and perfectly done.

Think of an Ice Breaker

Vegetable Cutter

A cutter that was simple but effective and a real boon for the cook and the kitchen maid.

Ice Breaker

What was life like before the advent of the refrigerator when it came to preserving food? Ice came in big blocks, hewn from ponds and glaciers. These were brought to the big houses and this dangerous looking tool broke the block into manageable sizes. Trying to guess what this gadget was used for would be a useful ice breaker at any present-day party!

Pea Fork

The ultimate in table manners! How embarrassing to be at the Victorian table and be chasing peas round a plate, or, worse still, have them go flying all over the floor. Someone realised the scale of the problem and came up with this pleasing solution. The peas are scooped up and nestle safely between the ridges before being brought delicately to the mouth, and the short prongs allow one to stab the odd one that gets away!

The Gourmet Pie Funnel

Funnel-style steam vents have been placed in the centre of fruit and meat pies during cooking since Victorian times; bird shapes came later.

Pie funnels are used to prevent pie filling from boiling up and leaking through the crust by allowing steam to escape from inside the pie. They also support the pastry crust in the centre of the pie so it does not sag in the middle, and are occasionally known as "crustholders." These were particular problems with older ovens, where the heat was not uniform across the pie—fan ovens have, to some extent, done away with the need for these funnels, especially in smaller pies.

Pie Funnels

Here is a small selection of the many printed funnels from the turn of the twentieth century, including two of the Gourmet Pie Cup, which has changed shape considerably whilst keeping its patent.

Boiled Eggs — How Do You Like Yours?

Boiled Egg Warmer

Getting boiled eggs to the table of the more affluent Victorian family, this lovely dish would have had a burner below that kept the eggs nice and warm, just ready to have with one's toasted soldiers at breakfast. Then it would be kippers, kidneys, chops—wealthy Victorians must have had ironclad digestive systems, as well as ironclads on every ocean on Earth.

Egg Boiler

Now, how do you like your eggs done? Soft and runny? Just nicely gooey in the middle of the yolk? Or solid and dependable?

This lovely kitchen gadget does the job. Just pop the eggs into the lip at the bottom and immerse in a pan of water. The whistle sounds as the water boils. Then count how many minutes from the whistle going off.

Just time to complete the *Times* crossword before the egg is ready!

Knife, Fork, and Spoon

Combination Cutlery Set

Possibly used in the military. A very easily assembled set, it slides together into a very neat whole. Ideal for round the camp fire.

Propellor Spoon

A very late nineteenth-century spoon that doubles the mixing action. As you beat the mixture, the agitator, in the shape of a propeller, goes in the opposite direction. Evidently it never really caught on, but would certainly have made soufflés rise and batter fly!

Combination Fork and Spoon

Not sure which is the fish knife? This clever little gadget allows you to sup soup, eat meat, and tackle a pudding all with one piece of cutlery. Dating from the early twentieth century, it may have been intended as an aid for the disabled, though surely separate eating irons would have been easier.

Beating, Rubbing, and Boiling the Egg

Egg Beater

Made in ceramic, there should be a metal insert which, when moved rapidly up and down, beats the egg into the required consistency.

Boiler and Warmer

Place on the stove and boil eggs in the bottom while keeping them warm in the top. Now, one egg or two?

Easy Egg Boiler

Ever had trouble removing the boiled egg from the pan? Here is a very effective solution. Also prevents cracking the egg when placing it into the pan.

Egg Cleaning Brush

When laid, the egg is usually dirty. This handy device made of sponge rubber on a curved wooden frame is the answer. Wet the sponge and off comes the dirt in one swipe.

Blowing Hot and Cold

Vacuum Flask

Vacuum flasks were a real breakthrough. This 1920s vacuum jug may not have been easily tucked away into your knapsack, but it is highly decorative and the spout looks a lot more efficient than those found on modern flasks.

Spoon Warmer

In the very best houses and restaurants in Victorian England nothing was left to chance. The complaint might not just have been, "Waiter, not only is this soup cold," but, "this soup spoon is cold, too." A decorative container filled with hot water to keep serving spoons and sauce ladles warm was the perfect solution. The earliest spoon warmers date from the 1860s. Of course, the waiter may have known better, "Sir, the soup you ordered is Gazpacho, a Spanish recipe, to be consumed chilled."

Just Toast

Telescopic Toasting Fork

Nearly every home had one of these telescopic toasting forks. And what lovely, crunchy toast they made. You just skewered the bread on the end of the prongs, extended the arm so you did not burn yourself, and held it before one of those lovely open fires with the embers glowing red—perfect!

Heating Rack for Toast

One of the difficulties enjoying toast is the speed it cools down. This was especially so in the larger house, where toast had to be carried up from the kitchen. So, why not keep the toast warm with this little paraffin heater? Of course, the contraption may burn the toast, and then there's the smell of the paraffin . . .

Toaster For Stove Top

Placed on top of primitive stoves back in the days of Victoria but also used in the Nissen huts of WWI, this extremely simple toaster does a mean slice. "Just pass us the butter and the Seville orange marmalade, there's a good chap!"

An Egg a Day . . .
Makes You Work, Rest, and Play

Egg Weigher and Grader

A simple weighing machine that will weigh two different bands and grade the lighter ones by shape and size. Cheap, cheerful, and ideal for the smallholder.

Victorian Egg Grader

By rolling the egg down the incline, the trap doors open based upon weight. Each little door has two counter-balance weights that can be adjusted by moving the lever arm up and down. The weights are even of different sizes, allowing for finer settings. The egg then falls through and is caught by hand and placed into different baskets. What about the ones that don't make the grade? Looks like they shoot off the end and . . . splat! Oh, dear, another fine mess . . .

Triple Egg Poacher

Each circular holder contained one egg for poaching. The beauty of this gadget is that when ready to place on the plate, a flick of the finger opens all three rings at once, presumably for three separate diners. Or is this a bit like the Weetabix test? Are you a two Weetabix and a three egg man?

So Butter Would Melt in Their Mouths

Butter and Spreader Set

Still a problem today: how to spread hard butter straight from the fridge. With sales of home refrigerators increasing in the '30s, these ingenious cutters and knives were just the answer. Simply by filling the handles of the gadgets with hot water, the cutting and spreading of butter becomes a doddle—a bit like a hot knife through butter, in fact!

Butter Melter

Filled with hot water, this wedge-shaped tool's main function was cutting slabs of butter, but it could also be used for ice cream and other foodstuffs coming from the "ice house." The ice house was found in large mansions. A deep hole or cellar would be packed with ice from local ponds in the winter, then all manner of foodstuffs could be kept fresh through the summer without going off. Of course, this all depended on the hard winters of late Victorian Britain—there would be no guarantee of ice on the ponds today.

Butter Shaper

All kinds of shapes could be made with this implement by just changing the patterned mould.

Supersize U

Two of these three kitchen gadgets were no doubt meant for the larger household or a hotel, but they are a reminder that large portions are not a modern concept. Most people had enough to eat but no more. Diets were often poor. Yet there were people who ate conspicuously large meals. A Victorian hotel breakfast today sounds horribly rich and gargantuan: porridge; bloaters; chop, devilled kidneys, and bacon; oysters; poached eggs; and tea and toast. Now, how many hours until lunch?

Baked Potato Maker

Spuds up! Do baked potatoes six at a time. For a large family or a café from the 1920s. But can we afford the butter, let alone the cheese or tuna mayo?

Toast Rack

When we first saw this extraordinary contraption from early in Victoria's reign, we would never have worked out this was a toast rack that fits on the side of the fire grate as a holder for toast being made on the fire until we researched the original patent. It looks more like something from outer space, but it does the job. Now, one slice or two?

Expanding Spatula

This really is one for the greasy spoon café or the American all-day breakfast diner. It doesn't matter how large the food frying in the pan, this device caters to all sizes; a quick flick of the fingers expands the business end to the required width. How many rashers did you say?

Poached Egg on Toast

Everything you need for the perfect start to the day or a teatime treat.

Poacher

A simple poacher, but with a spring handle. Crack the egg into the metal ring and place in boiling water. When poached, a flick of the lever allows it to slide smoothly onto the toast.

　　How do you like yours? Not too hard and the yolk rich and gooey in the middle?

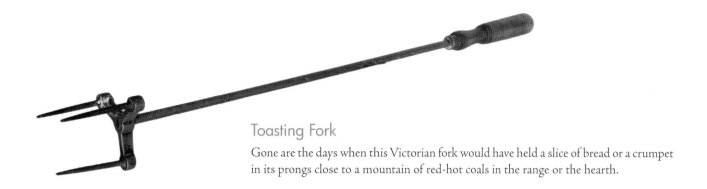

Toasting Fork

Gone are the days when this Victorian fork would have held a slice of bread or a crumpet in its prongs close to a mountain of red-hot coals in the range or the hearth.

Bottle Locks and Wine Stoppers

Stopping the butlers and servants getting to the drink. By the look of it, the male upper classes were obsessed with the idea that their best brandy or whisky would be filched.

Burns Bottle Lock

Using a key to lock the brandy from being tampered with by the servants whilst the squire is off shooting game. Late Victorian in age, Burns was the biggest suppliers of these security gadgets.

Bottle Stoppers

As we all know, wine goes off after being opened. These two patented stoppers allowed the elixir to be kept for another day.

Combination Whiskey Lock

Safe crackers would be needed to get into the best malt! This number combination lock is from Victorian times. Best not drink too much, or one might be too sozzled to remember the combination!

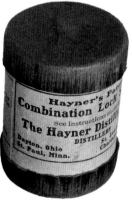

Stop It!

Security Brandy Bottle Cork

To stop any unauthorised imbiber, the owner of the house would replace the cork with this extraordinary contraption. It sealed the drink and could only be opened by the owner. Late Edwardian.

Metal Tantalus

This small metal cabinet has space for two bottles. What makes it different is its lock and key. The aim, as described in the literature of the time, was to stop unauthorised people drinking the contents, particularly "servants and younger sons of the aristocracy getting at the whisky!"

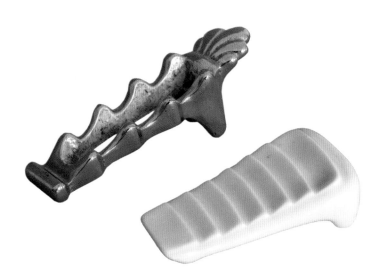

Table Manners

Soup Plate Lifters

Can you believe Victorians used these gadgets to lift the corner of their soup plates, little by little, until the last drop could be scooped up? It seems extraordinarily fastidious now but was the height of good table manners then.

Egg Cup

In beautifully turned wood, this egg turns into an egg cup. It was probably a campaign item taken to war by British army officers.

Mustard Dispenser

No garish yellow plastic squeezy bottle on a café counter, this beautifully designed Edwardian tableware allowed the diner, with just a push of the plunger, to dispense a hearty dollop of the finest English mustard.

Upstairs and Downstairs

Plate Holder and Server

Such a simple implement used by Victorians to hold the hot plate—kept warm in the oven—and to place it on the table. Its main use would be in more affluent homes where the butler would use it to serve dinner.

Returnable Dish

This must be a "ready meal" from the Edwardian era. When finished bring back the plate and get four pence—a lot in those days.

Spout Replacement

Perhaps not for the poshest houses, but an inventor thought he spotted a gap in the market. Teapot spouts are notoriously easy to break off. This rubber tubing and pot spout end were the answer. Not, we think, a great success—even the more pinched households might prefer to spend their hard-earned pennies on a new tea pot rather than ending up with an old one with a droopy spout!

Heinz Sauce Top

A clever advertising ploy. In the days before plastic bottles tops would easily go astray, so the Heinz company issued replacement tops to be kept in the cutlery draw, ready to stopper the ketchup.

Cool!

Cold Safe

This ceramic cover would be soaked and placed over the milk bottle to keep its contents from curdling. Very effective before refrigerators were commonplace. An essential piece of kit.

Coffee Cooler

This looks like a crazy idea. You filled the container with cold water, then you dropped it into the jug of hot coffee. But why?

Would blowing on the coffee not work as well? Or just wait a minute or two. Not to mention the danger of boiling hot coffee splashing out of the jug and over your skin as you drop the container—had the makers never heard of Archimedes?

Hygienic Milk Bowl

It is not entirely clear how this "Desideratum in Every Household" under the Dickensian sounding brand "Grimwade" actually did what it says. Dating from the Edwardian era, how did it stop milk slopping over? Surely a narrow top and a wider base would have prevented this, not the other way round. How did it stop flies walking into the milk? Could they not fly in?

Dated Seal Bottles

We rarely consider the development of the humble present day wine bottle. The fact is, they evolved from the late seventeenth century, with the onion shape of the 1726 bottle, through the period of the mallet-shaped bottles of 1757 and 1802, to the more or less familiar shape dated 1850. It was then that the mass produced, moulded bottle became the normal receptacle for wine. The reason for the name of a person or organisation being stamped onto a seal on early bottles is that they were free, hand-blown bottles individually made for the customers of the wine importers. The most famous seal bottle is one belonging to Samuel Pepys, now in the Museum of London.

It's a Lot of Codd's Wallop

Bottles containing sparkling water or lemonade have intrigued me for many years. The problem in the Victorian period was how to keep the gas in the bottle, as it tended to leak through the cork closures as they dried out. There were many inventions, the earliest of which, by a man called Hamilton, was a round bottom so it could never be stood up, which meant the liquid was in constant touch with the cork, thus stopping it from drying out. That then led to stands for Hamilton bottles so they could be presented at table.

In 1872, British soft drink maker Hiram Codd of Camberwell, London, designed and patented a bottle designed specifically to stop the gas escaping from the cork of carbonated drinks. It used a marble in the neck that was forced up by the pressure and thus stopped any gas escaping. When you wanted to drink, just a press and the marble was released and then held in a groove in the neck.

The phrase "what a lot of codd's wallop," meaning you're "talking a lot of gas," comes from this invention.

Later Round-Bottomed Lemonade Bottle

Hamilton Bottle

Codd's Bottles

Hamilton Bottle with Table Holder

The Brewing "Simple" Pot

A genuinely novel answer to the problems of stewed tea and leaves in the cup.

Simple but Perfect Teapot

The pot was made so it could stand either on its flat base or on its back, the "second base." The domed top covered half of the teapot, while the other half was covered by a lid that was constructed so it could not fall off when the pot was tilted forward. Inside, near the upper part of the teapot, a pierced tray was fixed across the pot, thus forming a compartment to hold the tea.

So how does it work? You put your tea leaves on the gauze infuser shelf. Then you stand the teapot upright and fill with hot water to the line just below the lid. To begin steeping the tea you lay the teapot all the way onto its back. When the desired strength has been reached you first tilt the pot to drain all the liquid from the leaves, then stand the teapot vertically again. The water is no longer bathing the leaves so the brew stays warm without becoming bitter. Simple, really.

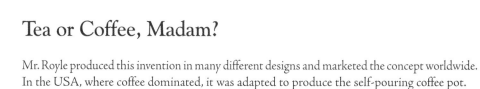

Tea or Coffee, Madam?

Mr. Royle produced this invention in many different designs and marketed the concept worldwide. In the USA, where coffee dominated, it was adapted to produce the self-pouring coffee pot.

Self-Pouring Teapot

In the 1880s, Mr. Royle of Manchester came up with this amazing idea of delivering the tea to the cup by using Archimedes' principle of displacement of liquid by an equal amount of air. Covering the hole in the lid when pressed caused the air to deliver one perfect cuppa through the spout. Elegant and functional.

Self-Pouring Coffee Pot

Oh, for a Nice Cup of Coffee

Siphon Balanced Coffee Brewer

Siphon coffee brewer pots were designed so you could put your grounds in the "brewing vessel" and pour the boiling water over the grounds. You would then light the burner under the "serving vessel," which would cause the air inside to expand, creating a partial vacuum that would syphon the brewed coffee into the serving vessel, where it would be kept warm.

Makes the modern cafetiere and the coffee machine look just a trifle dull. Now, latte or cappuccino?

TRAINS, BIKES, AND AUTOMOBILES

By the second half of the nineteenth century, travel for the masses was becoming a reality. There had been mass migrations before, and armies and navies had traversed the globe, but here at last was a chance for the ordinary man and woman to see beyond the village or the market town, to visit the big cities or go to the seaside. Here, too, was a chance for the city dweller to get out into the countryside, to visit friends and family, and also to take the sea air.

As much as the telegraph, telephone, and the wireless revolutionised communication, the railway and then the bicycle and motor car transformed travel for millions of people.

This is not so much about the engineering of steam locomotives or the development of the internal combustion engine as about all the gadgetry and paraphernalia that were soon added to the traveller's experience. The early motorist, in particular, seems to have struggled to find his or her way, and there were many clever attempts to make map-reading easier.

Mass transportation and later private means of transport played their part in a social revolution. Here are just a few of the gadgets that accompanied that change.

From Euston to Crewe in Comfort

"Oh, Mr Porter, what shall I do? I wanted to get off at Birmingham but they've taken me on to Crewe." The lack of lavatories on trains before corridor carriages was only one of the problems for the railway traveller. You could always read a book. Yet at first there were no lamps in carriages at all, and later oil lamps were not much better. So here are portable reading lamp kits. How safe it was wielding candles on a rocking train is anybody's guess.

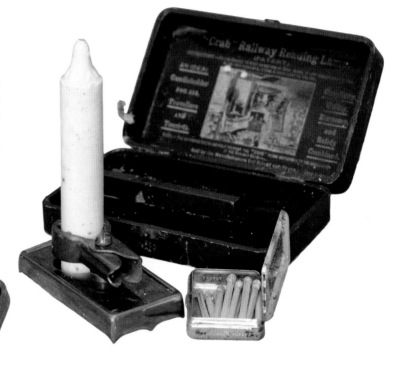

Easy Reading Railway Victorian Lamp

This neatly packed container of lighting components was designed to make the train journey more comfortable, as well as enable one to read one's magazine or book, ensuring as much safety as possible with the solid base and the well sprung clip. Minimising fire risk was essential. More people were killed by subsequent fire on trains than by railway crashes themselves.

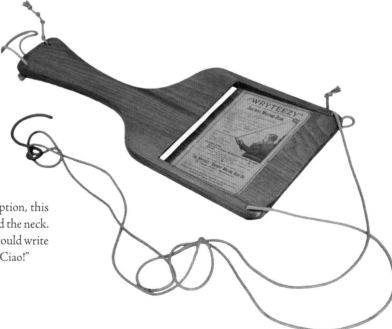

Write-Easy Table

As can be seen by the illustration attached to the contraption, this precursor to the laptop would have strings to attach around the neck. So, whilst travelling in a train carriage, the businessperson could write during their journey. "Hi! I'm out of the office at present. Ciao!"

When the Bulb Blows . . .

Tubular Metal Bulb Spare Pack

Cars at the beginning of the twentieth century were notorious for blowing their bulbs. Lighting technology was in its infancy, and the only answer was to carry a spare set of all bulbs. Many upmarket manufacturers such as Rolls Royce and Martini provided tubular metal box packs like this one with emergency bulbs ready to hand.

Getting the Bike on the Road

Bicycle Lamp

What's different with this lamp from the '30s is the integrated mirror, allowing you to see what is happening behind—might be useful on today's roads!

Bicycle Bell

The difference in this bell is that it has no lever; you have to twist the top of the bell to get it to ring. Maybe not the most clever nor the safest of inventions.

Cyclists Clips

An early Victorian pair of cycle clips and a very neat set of clips from the 1940s to stop your turn-ups getting caught in the chain.

Bike Air Pump

After the dreaded puncture, and having made the repair, the intrepid 1930s cyclist would have used this solid hand pump to get back on the road.

"The Plus Four" 1920s Sat-Nav

Route Indicator

Even ninety years ago, people were innovating products to allow drivers to find their way around Britain. Made to be worn on the wrist for easy checking, this delightful contraption uses tiny map scrolls. As you drive you turn the knobs on the side of the watch and you follow the prescribed route, which at the same time gives you the mileage between each town marked.

One snag is what if you didn't want to start from London and you didn't want to go to Bournemouth, Eastbourne, or Margate? Like many modern devices, the money was to be made not from selling you the initial watch and scrolls, but from charging you exorbitantly for new route scrolls.

Cleverly, it also doubles as a golf scorer on the back of the scrolls, so if you ever did find your way to Royal St. George's you could enjoy a round of golf with old Biffy, assuming good old Biffy had also made it there with one of these!

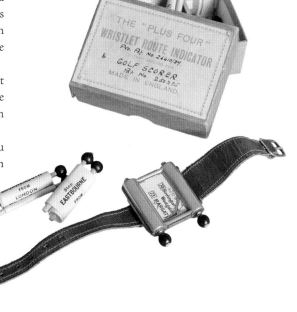

Extroverts Only

Here are three items from 1900 through the 1930s for the man about town. Whether rolling along in an early motor car, driving like a pioneer racer, or spending one's evenings in pool halls or at the billiards table, these gadgets made a statement.

Auto-Specs

With early cars having little or no windscreen protection goggles were a necessity, but these autospecs are a little different from ordinary goggles of the time. We think they may have been for night driving, both protecting the eyes and reducing the glare from oncoming cars.

Metal Arm Bands

Worn in films by snooker players in gambling dives in the '30s, they did of course hold up your sleeves whilst making that vital pot.

Exhaust Hooter

Let them know you are coming! This extraordinary contraption has a silencer box and a tuba horn! You literally made music—or a racket!—as you went along. We assume this was not factory fitted, but was an accessory for the Edwardian boy racer. It works: blowing into it does indeed produce a blast of sound.

Mr. Toad's Necessary Accessories

Carbide Car Light

Water is allowed to drip into the chamber containing the calcium carbide, creating a powerful beam for the vehicle in the dark.

Car Note Taker

Affixed to the dashboard, the gadget contained note paper, allowing the driver to jot down ideas or shopping lists as he or she bowled along—like being on your mobile whilst driving, and probably even more dangerous!

Car Burglar Alarm

Auto crime is nothing new. In the late '40s, attempts were made to stop the theft of vehicles with a range of different alarms. This is one of the more bizarre. You fasten the gadget to your spark plugs. If the engine is started up it gives a loud bang and there is a large puff of smoke—just don't forget to disconnect before you set off in the car yourself!

Tyre Measure

When the tyre first arrived on the scene there was no standard measure. The mechanic could run this wheel around the rim and so find the size. A vital piece of kit in days when punctures were commonplace.

Finding Your Way

The Roller Map

The aristocracy, when having the pleasure of driving, required a mapping system to reach their destination using this stylish gadget. This amazing leather-cased, roller-based contraption surely lived up to their expectations.

The Webster Motor Map was based on the mechanism of early cameras. It used rollers similar to those that held photographic film, but instead a rolled map of each area was placed in the geared slots and turned as the journey progressed. When you ran off the map you inserted another roller. Edwardian.

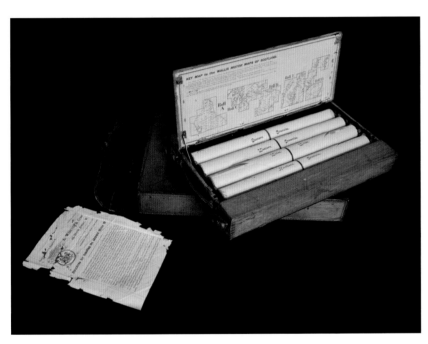

What! Not Lost Again?

Scrolling Mechanical Map

The idea of the mechanical, scrolling map continued to be developed. Looking like a modern smartphone or e-reader, this plastic map reader is from the 1950s.

You looked up the section number, pressed it, and that bit of the UK appeared. It works on both sides: one side for southern Britain and one for northern Britain. Rather clever, even if the maps are a trifle small.

Pocket Gambling Game

If you really were lost, you could always pull out this ingenious game. Real betting at calculated odds on which three-letter word will appear when the box is shaken and opened. Not one for the children to use, and be careful you don't lose your shirt before you reach your destination!

Putting Your Foot Down

Ladies' Heel Protector

From the 1920s, this simple concept was successfully marketed for use by ladies whilst driving. A straightforward gadget to solve a real problem, especially when going in your very best court shoes—might it still have a use today?

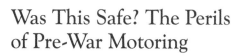

Was This Safe? The Perils of Pre-War Motoring

Anti-Headlight Dazzle

We have no idea how it works, but the intention is to prevent being dazzled by oncoming traffic with their lights full on—was it before the advent of dipped headlights?

Frost Shields

Surely one of the most useless and dangerous driving accessories ever invented, this 1930s frost shield is so tiny we can only think the Peerless Novelty Company was having a joke at the motorist's expense.

Steering Wheel Warmers

Place these on the rim of the steering wheel, plug the wires into the cigarette lighter socket on the dash board, and you can drive along in the winter with warm hands or run the battery completely flat—not a big success in the 1920s.

When One Door Opens . . .

Railway Carriage Key

Older carriages locked with this type of key can still be found, especially on the heritage railways. Railway employees had such keys, but this one fits away neatly into the handle, and there is no railway company insignia. Might this have been a director's key for the first-class compartments? Can any reader cast further light on this natty gadget?

Automobiles

Tyre Gauge

Not so long ago every motorist would have one of these pressure gauges in their pocket or at least in the glove compartment. A simple spring device, the needle is inserted in the valve and the pressure is read from the barrel. This example is dated around 1950. Younger readers may be less familiar with tyre gauges, but punctures and soft or flat tyres were a common occurrence back then.

Petrol Anti-Theft Device

Siphoning petrol still goes on. This American device from the 1950s took a belt and braces approach to stopping the theft. You put this surprisingly large spring down the filler tube and that was that. Love the name "Auntie Siphon."

Getting to the Top

The Coachman's Ladder

This looks for all the world like just a few pieces of wood held together in a bundle by a leather belt, but undo the buckle and give it a gentle pull and all is revealed. The ladder opens to its full height and the rungs, hidden inside the bundle, appear as if by magic.

This brilliantly engineered coachman's ladder is from the Victorian period. By then railways were arriving, but many coaches still ran into the middle of the nineteenth century.

Never Be Caught Short

Portable Carriage Commode

When the Victorian aristocracy embarked on a long journey in their horse-drawn carriages, the problem of relieving oneself in a more or less civilised way would be solved by using Mr. R. Wiss's portable toilet, which would be carried on the back of the carriage.

The decorated, glazed bowl is delightfully sweet. One trusts that no one mistook it for a dining dish, given its real purpose!

Bertie, Are You Sure You Know the Way?

Magnifier Glass Slide Map

This sturdy and beautifully constructed Edwardian contraption was clearly intended as the answer to paper maps. Every part of the UK is printed on glass slides. As you bowl along, you place the next slide into the frame and turn down the magnifier to get a magnified image of the roads. We wondered why this was such a rare example—it clearly never sold. Apart from the weight of lugging the bulky box about there is the problem of having to stop every few miles to adjust the position of the lens or change slides. Not for the first time the Edwardians had come up with an over-elaborate solution.

OFFICE AND SCHOOL

Just as the home and kitchen were gradually mechanised, so, too, was the office. The Dickensian vision of Bob Cratchit clerks and scribes bent over desks with quill pen and ink was to be replaced by the Orwellian vision of row upon row of female typists and boffins in the background with their computers and calculators. Yet gadgetry in the office was mainly for the good, even if it didn't always feel that way.

Here are the early attempts to produce mechanical calculators that were at least as efficient as the abacus. Here, too, are the contraptions that never quite made it in the commercial world.

The changes brought by invention seem to have affected the schoolroom least during this period, yet here, too, inventors were hard at work trying to come up with something really useful. The school desk, methods of teaching, and the classroom may have changed only a little during the century and a half covered by this collection, but at least the gadgets in the pencil case and the school satchel could be a little bit novel.

Look out especially for that harbinger of mass marketing and junk mail, the automated envelope sealing machine.

Talking Your Way to the Top

Dictaphone

The idea of a portable dictating machine goes back a long way. This wonderful looking device was moveable, if not actually portable. Only snag was, to re-use a cylinder, you needed another apparatus to shave off the old wax and re-coat it.

You recorded through the mouthpiece onto a wax cylinder. The recording could be played back by the secretary when needed. Notice it has room to store up to six cylinders, though one memo might well take up a whole cylinder.

Stapleless Stapler

Somehow the inventor of this machine found a way of cutting and folding the edges of sheets of paper so they hold together. First developed in Japan in the 1920s. Maybe not the roaring success anticipated, as staples are still the norm today!

Automatic Gumming Machine

The roll of sticky paper goes into the machine, the cogs turn, and the paper rolls through the reservoir of water and comes out ready to adhere to the envelope.

Automating the Office

Copying Machine

Even in the late nineteenth century, the ability to copy the written word was vital, but without the need to employ banks of Dickensian scribes and copy clerks. In this very basic copier the wet ink of the original is transferred onto a special paper which is then used to print a copy on a new sheet of paper.

Pawnbrokers Reciept Machine

This invention saved time and money for the owner of the shop; it writes the receipts by pen automatically in quadruplicate! A real sign of how busy pawnbrokers were, as well as a beautiful example of Victorian engineering in miniature. But why so many copies? Well, if you needed to see "uncle," you would need a receipt, one to go with the item, one for invoicing, and one for the taxman! Yes, times may change, but there are, of course, only two things certain in life . . .

Waxing Lyrical

For centuries sealing wax ensured documents were kept secret or arrived safely without tampering. An impression in the sealing wax could also be used to verify the sender's identity, for example with a signet ring, "It really is a message from King John!"

The Romans used bitumen for this purpose. Later, wax was used to seal "letters close," what we would now call notelets, and, from the sixteenth century, envelopes. No doubt letters were still tampered with, but at least a wax seal meant you needed more than just some steaming kettles!

Seal Remover

You have in your hand Aunt Jane's last will and testament. The whole family is gathered round expectantly. Only a wax seal stands between you and a tidy fortune. "Pass me my seal chisel." The seal lifts cleanly from the parchment. You scan the will, "I leave my entire estate to . . . the Seamen's Mission."

A Victorian gadget that no doubt unlocked many a tragic message.

Paper Letter Seals

By the 1920s, gummed envelopes had largely made wax seals redundant for letters, but these cheery, fun envelopes used the idea of the seal to brighten up your day—a bit like those over-the-top greetings and emoticons in emails and texts.

Sealing Wax

The wax comes in sticks and could be purchased at most stationery stores throughout the Victorian and Edwardian period.

Lead in Your Pencil

Modern pencils do not contain metallic lead, as the "lead" of the pencil is actually a mix of finely ground graphite and clay powders. The hardness of the pencil is determined by the amount of clay in the mixture: the less clay, the softer the pencil. The quality of the lead is determined by how finely the graphite and clay is ground: cheaper pencils have less finely ground mixtures and, hence, the lead is more likely to break, leading to the frustration of having to sharpen it again and again, as well as muttering, "False economy!"

Pencil Extension

No need to throw away those pencil stubs: use them right down to the last with this pencil extender! Doubles as a letter opener.

Magnetic Pencil

Making sure you always have a note taker by the phone, this '50s invention has a magnetic plate you place on the table by the telephone. The steel casing of the pencil sticks to the plate, ensuring you never have to say, "Hang on a minute while I find something to write with."

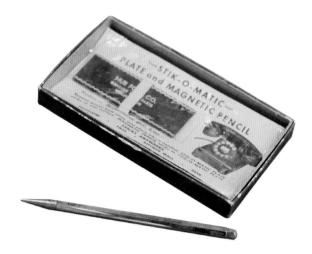

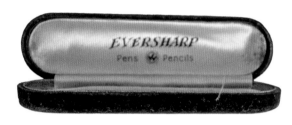

Eversharp Pencil

A clever take on the propelling pencil. The lead is placed inside the barrel. Every time you push it forward, the razor-sharp nozzle sharpens it to the finest of points.

Pantograph

A delightful give-away from the soap manufacturer Rinso from the 1940s. It has a variety of points to pin the Pantograph, allowing for a range of shapes to be drawn. One of many sales gimmicks for children, but with a message for their parents.

Inky Fingers

The ability of most people to write transformed society. For all its drudgery and inequality, the development of elementary schools for all children was one of the great successes of Victorian society. Whole industries developed to deal with the demands of a more literate population. The steel nib industry alone, based in the Black Country in the West Midlands, employed thousands of people.

Travelling Inkwell

In the days of using "dip pens" (a piece of wood with a nib on the end), ink would be needed wherever you were. Fountain pens were still a luxury in Edwardian times, so this travelling inkwell would have been just the job on the train or in the boarding house.

Self-Filling Inkwell

In the Victorian period, many hundreds of patents were filed to deal with how ink is delivered to the pen. This example keeps filling the pot on the right from the reservoir without overflowing.

Inkwell Filler

Some of us might just remember being the "ink monitor," the person in class who had the honour of filling everyone's wells in the classroom. Notice the "drip catcher" at the base of the funnel.

"Anything in the Post, Dear?" "Just Junk Mail and Begging Letters."

Automatic Envelope Sealer

How did it all start? Well, this machine, an automatic envelope sealer, was a big step on the way not only to automating the office, but to that daily flutter of circulars through the letter box.

This machine is from the Edwardian era. Mind, think of all the gummy lips and fingers it would have prevented.

Automating at least some aspects of the postal service allowed mail order firms to expand rapidly. Throughout the late nineteenth and early twentieth century, mail order was the most important means of many people shopping for larger or more specialist items, especially in places like Canada, Australia, and the USA. A bit like the impact of Internet shopping, in fact!

We'll Get this Licked if We Stick Together!

If like me you never liked licking envelopes, you'll know why from the earliest days of sending mail people have sought machines to do the job for us. Of course, ever since paper was invented there has been a need to find ways of making one sheet adhere to another, but the arrival of a full postal service made that even more imperative. Today self-seal envelopes and e-mails are making the problem obsolete, but here are two early solutions.

Full Sheet Gummer

Placing glue inside the drum, a plain sheet of paper would pass through the roller, covering the whole of one side of the sheet with glue which, when dry, was ready for use.

Notice the lovely Victorian decoration on this Allen's machine.

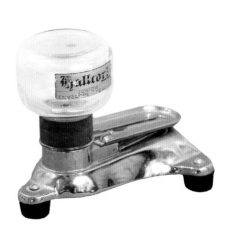

Single Envelope Gluer

The bottle was filled with water, then the edge of the pre-gummed envelope was pulled through. Moistened, the envelope was closed by hand. For the smaller office from the 1920s.

"Take This Down . . ."

Short Hand Trainer Characters

These finely crafted wooden figures look like an ancient language; in a way, that is precisely what they are. They were intended for teaching Pitman shorthand. The figures, only some of which are illustrated, were used to draw on a blackboard. They could be altered so every Pitman symbol could be produced in large, easy-to-copy figures on the board.

If any reader was taught Pitman this way and can cast further light on their use we would be delighted to hear from them.

It Just Doesn't Add Up!

Cardboard Mechanical Multiplier

Before the computer and calculator there were mechanical inventions to do the sums. Were Victorians and Edwardians better at mental arithmetic? Probably, but they were not without a myriad of gadgets to help get the right answer. The systems based on cardboard, such as the Children's Encyclopaedia, were a favourite way of advertisers reaching the school population, and notice the promise to explain the whole world for a half-penny a day.

Mechanical Calculators

Both these patents are from the beginning of the twentieth century. The innovative German machine on the right was designed for addition. The Sterling currency model has nine chains and can add up to £99,999 19s 11d—way beyond the sums most people would have to spend.

Making a Point

Swan Pencil Sharpener

A serious bit of kit—Victorian heavy engineering.

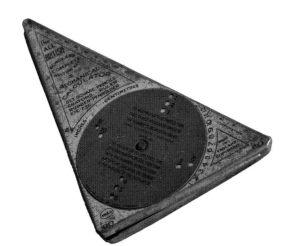

Pen and Pencil Box with Calculator

From the 1930s, this school mathematics set for the rather more privileged child has everything that the budding engineer might need. No doubt many a proud Grandpa and Grandma wrapped a set such as this for little Henry or Henrietta before their first day at grammar school.

Pencil Sharpener

An exciting pencil pointer with the cutting blades on the outside of the machine—mind your fingers!

The Stamp of Authority

Stapleless Paper Fasteners

This amazing invention, designed we believe back in the '20s, uses an ingenious cutting and folding technique to hold sheets of paper together. This is an original Japanese version, but the method can be seen in use in a slightly later American model. A good idea that did not last; the stapler won and rules to this day.

Stapler

Richard Gatling was a prolific American inventor. The machine gun was just one of his ideas—his most notorious and enduring. He did not invent the cartridge stapler, but this intriguing stapler was made by Gatling in the late 1800s. The fact it, too, looks dangerous, like the sting in the tail of a scorpion, is accidental, but adds piquancy to its charm—rattling out staples as fast as bullets.

Stamp Applicator

A roll of stamps would be inserted into the contraption and each push of the plunger affixes one stamp onto each envelope—licks licking them!

Timing Stamp

As the letters and documents landed in the office mailroom or on the desk, this stamp would mark them to the minute—no doubt reducing arguments over the time taken to complete a transaction.

Tidying Paper

Crinkle Fastener

This machine works on the basis of indenting papers to stay together, like perforation marks. Unfortunately, it does not give a permanent hold and the invention was not very successful. From the early '50s.

Stab Fastener

Many of us will be familiar with receiving paperwork and stabbing it onto a nail. Whether any serious injuries ever came about from people hitting their hand or head on the tip of the nail—perhaps through frustration with the accounts department—we do not know, but this device from the 1920s was a safer version of the good old nail.

Newspaper Clips

A simple system of keeping your newspaper pages in some kind of order. Back in the '30s, before tabloids, most daily papers were broadsheets and handling them with dignity was difficult; this clip solved the problem.

Seal, Scrap, and Polish

Scrap Roller

Victorians loved keeping scrap books, and this patent roller allowed them to be compiled in a jiffy. Choose your cutting, letter, or picture and just roll away!

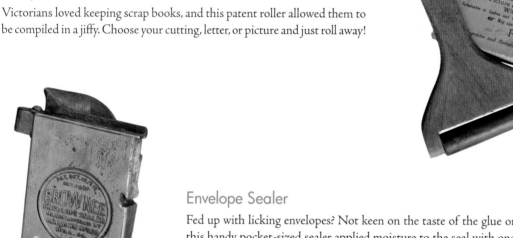

Envelope Sealer

Fed up with licking envelopes? Not keen on the taste of the glue on your tongue? No problem; this handy pocket-sized sealer applied moisture to the seal with one quick movement.

Kiwi Polish Notebook

A useful advertising give-away, in this case from Britain's leading brand of shoe polish. As you pulled out more and more of the notebook you were reassured that "Kiwi," the quality boot polish, reflected your smart appearance.

Pencils Rule, Ok

Multi-Purpose Ruler

Not only could you draw vertical straight lines, but also horizontal ones in the small apertures on either side. All this plus a sharp edge that allows you to tear paper easily and accurately.

Bank Pad

This rather charming gadget was aimed at the smart yet prudent 1930s citizen. Just jot down each purchase and keep a tally of your remaining balance on the right-hand side. Not an automated calculator, but a great way to keep spending in check—not for the spendthrift!

Calendar and Calculator Pencils

The propelling pencil goes multi-functional! The lower one is from the 1940s and incorporates a monthly calendar to keep track of the day and the date—you reset it at the beginning of each month. The upper one is from the 1950s and is very clever—a slide rule on a pencil, ideal for the student.

Calculator Pencil

The Entire World
on a Page

Page Turner - Geographical Give-Away

The late Victorians went to great lengths to find promotional ideas that linked with their customers' business. The page turner illustrated not only gives you a calendar but a map of the world. The company advertising its wares is the "Eastern Telegraph Company." These substantial page-turners were for use as bookmarks and turners for the large account ledger books of the period.

Portable Duplicator

Duplicating Machine

The spirit duplicator was invented in 1923 by Wilhelm Ritzerfeld. "Spirit" refers to the alcohols used as solvents in the inks on these machines. Many a school secretary or charity organiser will have felt a little woozy or even tipsy after using one of these in a confined space!

The duplicator used two-ply sheets: one was typed or written on and the second had a wax layer, which when cut by the pen or the typewriter made a template through which the "ink" could be rolled onto the paper beneath.

This lovingly preserved version is fully portable. With no drum, it would have been a laborious procedure to roll out every single copy. Nevertheless, in the days before photocopiers it would get the job done, if rather slowly.

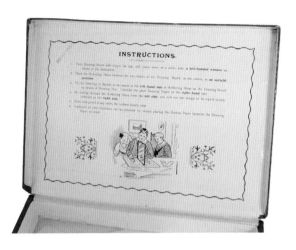

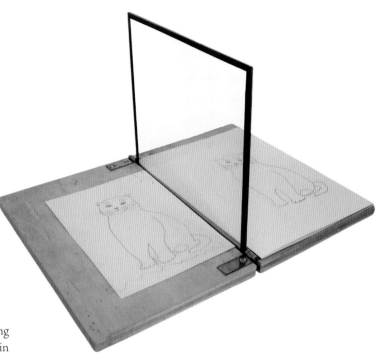

To Draw to One's Attention

Drawer and Copier

An interesting Edwardian system of copying original items using a glass reflector, giving an image of the original on the plain paper on the other side of the glass. Delightful for children.

Magnifier, 1920s

This magnifying glass and stand allowed the fine detail of small items to be copied with both hands free, for example if copying lettering.

Curve Drawer

Before Computer Aided Design drawing perfect curves was tricky. This invention, used by Victorian draftsmen, was just the job.

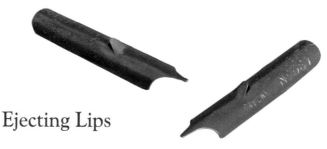

Ejecting Lips

Lip Ejecting Nibs

When "stick pens" were the way to write in the Victorian era, the production of nibs was a massive industry based in Birmingham and the Black Country. This very simple patent made George Hughes loads of money by just having a piece of metal jutting out from the top side of the nib. When you needed to change the nib, a sharp pull against the desk top removed it without soiling your fingers with ink. Quite one of the simplest yet most effective patents in the whole collection.

Compendium of Writing

An ideal birthday present for the Edwardian school pupil. This clever metal compendium set held a pen with nib, a pencil, and a knife sharpener. It was designed to be hung on a ribbon round the child's neck. Dated around 1910.

Envelope Water Applicator

Another Problem Licked

Envelopes have been a common product in the form we know today since the middle of the nineteenth century. Originally glue had to be applied to each envelope to seal it, then a gum that worked when moistened was applied by machine to every flap. That left the problem of how to apply the water. Clerks and office workers would soon tire of licking each envelope, so many inventors jumped in with devices to solve the problem. Today even this problem is passing into history with self-sealing envelopes and e-mails.

Envelope Water Applicator

Gum Label Applicator

The "Knowall"

These chart wheels or volvelles date from the 1930s. The four examples here show the range of subjects covered by these information machines, from the sixpenny calculator advertising the *Daily Mirror* to animals of the world.

They fulfilled an educational need in addition to promoting a brand, for example, with simple mathematics on one side of the "knowall" and geography on the reverse.

The co-op produced the lovely wild flowers and wild bird wheels, giving information on identification. These were probably given away to schools.

In their simple way, these volvelles were the Internet of their day, and, many might think, a good deal friendlier, if not quite as fast.

Those Happy School Days!

Compendium of Writing and Calculation

Containing rulers, nib pen, and calculator, all in its own easy-to-carry box. From the 1940s.

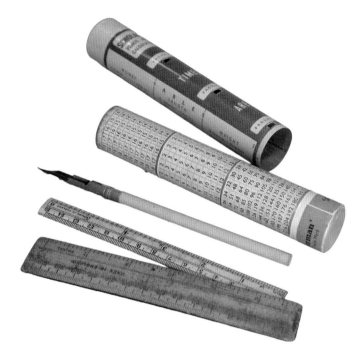

Chalk Holder

This is one for the music teacher. Just put chalk into each of the five "fingers," pull across the blackboard, and, presto, music lines ready for all those crotchets and quavers!

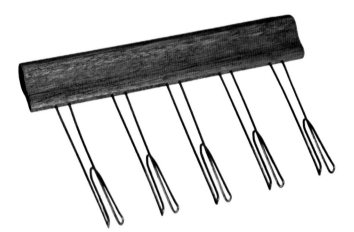

The 1916 Children's Calculator

This ingenious geometrical device did multiplication: a ready reckoner up to your twelve times table. Just move the feet to the two numbers you want multiplied and the correct answer appears in the aperture the animal is holding. But, I hear you say, in my day every child knew their tables backwards. Don't tell me the child of 1916 actually cheated by using one of these calculators?!

BABES AND CHILDREN

Large families and infant mortality were common in Victorian and Edwardian times. The need to provide bread winners, the fear of being left in penury in old age, and inadequate means of birth control all led to children numbering into the teens in many cases. As poverty was reduced and infant mortality rates came down the number of children also fell, even before the contraceptive pill. Increasing affluence and improved healthcare and sanitation had a marked effect on family size.

Those children who did survive—and that was by far the majority in the nineteenth century—had the same needs and desires as children today. Toys, games, and diversions of every kind were invented to entertain babes and children.

Helping mothers cope with babies was another area open to gadgets of all sorts. Here are just a few examples of gizmos and contraptions designed to improve the lot of the nursing mother.

There are also reminders of the perils that had to be faced, not least two examples of babies' and children's gas masks in the collection, when the fear of chemical warfare on the home front in World War II was all too real.

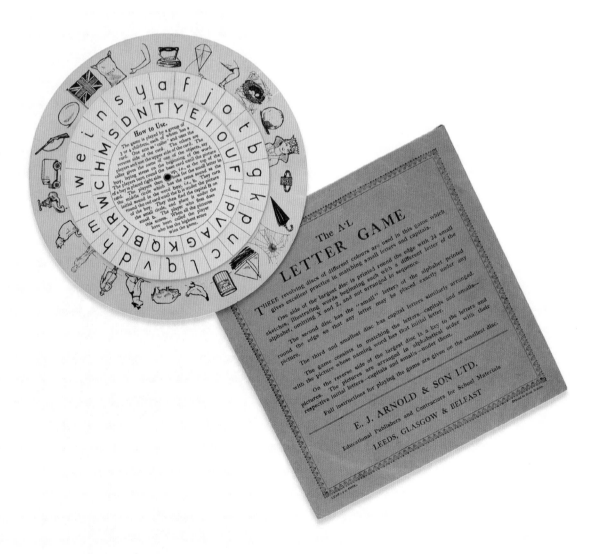

Now, Stop Sucking Your Thumb and Don't Play with Your Food!

Thumb-Sucking Stopper

It seems a cruel instrument to stop a poor child from having the satisfaction of sucking his/her thumb, but it no doubt worked. An alternative method was to cut the thumb off completely, but we understand only the sternest Victorian parent went that far.

Child's Food Masticator

To make sure food was easy to swallow, this instrument would mash it to an edible state, and woe betide the recalcitrant child should Papa have this fiendish device within reach. Or were Victorian parents more loving than many have led us to believe?

Food Warmer and Night Light

Sadly the burner is missing, but this lovely apparatus kept the food warm overnight and allowed the nanny to see what she was doing. Yet another example of the fondness of the Victorian inventor for multi-functional gadgets.

In the Balance

Baby Balance

Today everything has become digital, but in yesteryear babies were weighed with this simple spring balance, complete with baby hammock. Light and easy for the midwife to carry from home to home.

Baby Hammock

There is a lovely laid back feel to this simple woven string basket—the baby fits perfectly, gurgling, not crying, as it is weighed. This particular version is from the late 1940s, although similar products have been on the market from the end of the nineteenth century.

Babes in War and Peace

"Besco" Child's Shampoo Eye Shield

Not so much a case of smoke gets in your eyes as soap gets in your eyes and very unpleasant it is, too. To avoid all the problems, here is a simple idea from the 1950s to keep mum and baby happy with fewer tears.

Child's Gas Mask from WWII

When the war started, the threat of gas attacks on civilians was taken very seriously. Every adult and child was issued gas masks and this respirator was specially produced for young children.

Nanny, Baby, and Infants

Nanny Broach

A real piece of jewellery that was worn by nannies. It contained cotton and a needle to do repairs whilst on the job.

Blanket Securers

These clips would hold blankets around the baby securely so they would always be snug and warm.

Children's Plate Warmer

To keep the food warm hot water was poured into the tin base of the plate through the spout.

Nipple Shields

When women suffered from sore nipples, it was thought putting this device on the breast would protect the nipple and reduce the pain. However, what was not realised at the time is that the baby feeds from the breast, not just the nipple, and these devices would actually prevent the baby from getting milk and probably provide an unpleasant sensation for the baby, who was expecting to feel his mother's softness rather than a metallic object.

Hand-Operated Breast Pump

Mechanical Breast Pump

Here is another, almost-new, breast pump. We believe this pump is from the late nineteenth century, from a slightly later date than the previous example. These mechanical breast pumps would have been in use in hospitals, on maternity wards, and by midwives, as well as in the mansions of the wealthy.

Breast pumps are not really pumps as such, but the action of the pumping movement triggers a response to allow milk to flow.

As so often for the period, an amazingly well-engineered item and in a mighty fine box.

Nits and Lice, Dangers and Solutions

Nits are the eggs deposited by a female head louse that are glued firmly to the base of the hair shaft, close to the scalp, where it is humid enough for them to develop properly. After seven days, an immature head louse (nymph) will emerge from the egg. After shedding their skin (moulting) three times, head lice nymphs become sexually mature adult head lice.

WWI Louse Poster

Issued in 1918. Possibly used in army barracks to inform the soldiers of the dangers of the louse—as if they wouldn't be aware of them already—and knowledge on how to remove them.

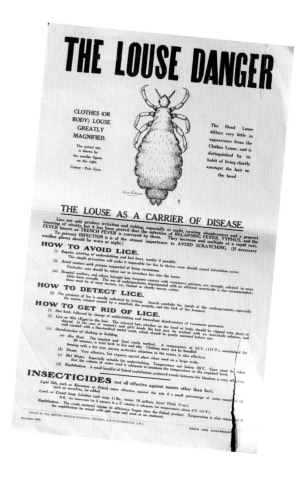

Nit Comb

The problem of nits being passed from student to student at school exists to this very day. Nit combs have been the solution since Victorian times. Here is a lovely double-sided comb from 1910.

Learning How to Spell

Letter Game

A game for parents to play with their children, but how did it work? We cannot for the life of us make out how it was to be used from the instructions. Can anyone familiar with the products of E. J. Arnold, a respected Leeds educational publisher, help? From the 1940s.

Speaking Children's Farm Book

Long before today's plethora of electronic speaking books and toys for children, innovative Victorian toy makers managed to create sound by the simple pull of a string alongside each of the animal pictures. The realistic moo of the cow or the bray of the horse was linked to the story alongside the pictures of the animals. Charming and ingenious.

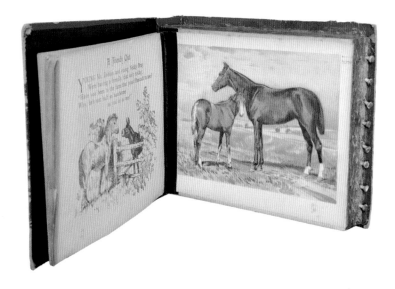

Squeeky Animal Book

A very rare example of a toy that gave a great deal of happiness to toddlers back in the nineteenth century. There were other attempts to create sounds mechanically before the electronic age, but this ingenious rubbing together of wires and paper managed to produce a surprisingly authentic imitation of each farmyard animal.

Hubble, Bubble . . .

Double Bubble Blower

All children love blowing bubbles, so to be able to produce bubbles within bubbles is doubly bubbly fun. What's intriguing about this children's toy is that it's all down to the wooden valve that you attach to the straw. The instructions make it clear, however, that it needs good breathing control. From 1918, a year when children everywhere might have been especially glad of novelty and distraction.

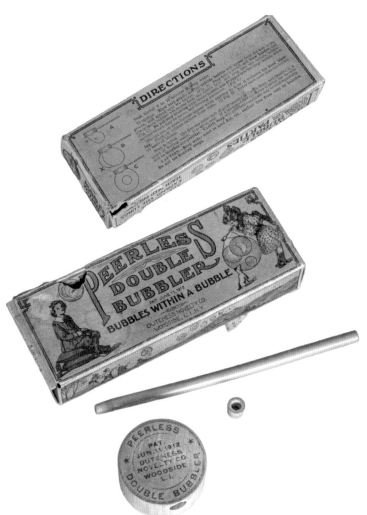

Amusing the Kids

Colour Retention

The Children's Encyclopaedia was loved by thousands of youngsters from its inception in 1908 until the final edition in 1964. This card explained the basis for light and colour retention by the nerve cells of the eye with the simple experiment of looking hard at the animals, only to discover they are still there when you turn the card over.

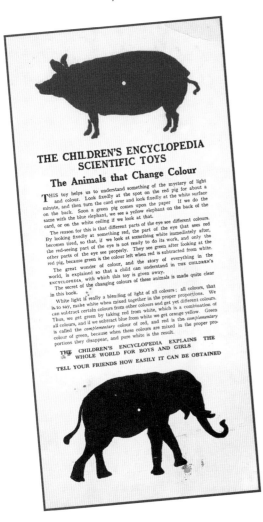

Dancing Charlie

From the mid-'40s, this simple cardboard puppet gave pleasure to thousands of youngsters. It often mystified those watching how Charlie seemed to dance unaided. The trick was a simple piece of cotton attached to a chair and pulled by the owner. It worked best when the cotton was the same colour as the background.

Spinning Top

The classic children's spinning top. Give the plunger a hearty push and the top twirls around the floor like a ballet dancer. This Victorian example makes a lovely whistling noise as it spins.

Infant Walker

Walkers are used to this day to enable children to find their legs. This simple walker, held by a wooden bar, is from the 1940s. Now steady, careful—oh, well done!

Sherlock Holmes Game

Parker Brothers', the American games manufacturer, brought out this card game linked to the famous English detective. It had a marketing head start, as everyone in the world knew of Sherlock Holmes's exceptional deductive abilities. A great commercial success: "Elementary, my dear Watson"—even if he never did say that in the books!

ESSENTIAL ACCESSORIES

Nowhere can a collection of gadgets and thingamajigs be more relevant than with accessories: those necessary bits and bobs without which life, or at least a good wardrobe, cannot function properly. The inventors and gadgeteers were at their busiest in the field of accessories. Here there is a little something for everyone.

You would think a coat hanger was a coat hanger and that would be that. Not a bit of it. If designing a better mouse trap was really at the front of the inventor's mind, then devising a better coat hanger was not far behind. Here there is an array of hangers: telescopic, folding, portable—all of them designed to keep one's clothes in perfect condition.

In the Victorian period boots and shoes were a constant worry. With muddy roads, ploughed fields, and horse muck everywhere, the Victorian lady and gent were endlessly trying to keep their feet warm and dry. Here, too, is an area for the gadget and the knacky accessory. When collars, especially on men's shirts, were detachable and replaceable, there were many contraptions to attach them or straighten them. Even the humble comb was reinvented.

So take a look inside the world of the accessory and the knick-knack.

Cleaning, Combing, Brushing, and Hanging

Moustach Brush and Comb

An integrated tool for the Edwardian gentleman to be able to do all the titivating his upper lip deserved. Note the lovely little mirror so he could make sure both ends of the 'tache were precisely symmetrical!

Clothes Brush and Hanger

What a handy asset to have along with your luggage. Brush the jacket and then hang it in the wardrobe—and the hanger is telescopic to fit any width garment. This is one of the gadgets that really is a gem of inventiveness: neat, clever, crisp design, and well made. Even better, it has a clear and practical function—ten out of ten!

Electrostatic Clothes Brush

This 1930s product, with its special lint dust pick-up, was the predecessor of the K-Tel brush-o-matic that was advertised on TV back in the 1980s.

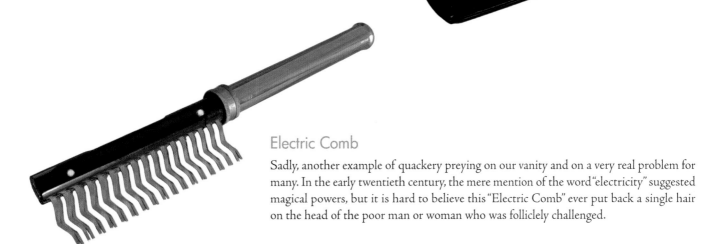

Electric Comb

Sadly, another example of quackery preying on our vanity and on a very real problem for many. In the early twentieth century, the mere mention of the word "electricity" suggested magical powers, but it is hard to believe this "Electric Comb" ever put back a single hair on the head of the poor man or woman who was folliclely challenged.

If the Shoe Fits . . .

Shoe Tree

We should all use a shoe tree to maintain the shape of our footwear, but in the age of trainers and sneakers how many do?

Shoe Warmers

A simple pair of stoneware shoe warmers from the turn of the twentieth century. Place in the boot, pour in hot water, cork, and the footwear is beautifully warm and snug in the morning. Just don't forget to remove the shoe warmers before wearing!

Shoe Studs and Protectors

Placed on the base of the boot, segs extend the life of soles for years. Better still, Blakey's segs are still made in Leeds to this day.

Intergrated Shoe Brush and Cloth

Handy cloth, brush, and shiner all in one.

Ouch!

Bunion Shoe Stretcher

Victorians certainly knew how to design contraptions to frighten the patient. This allowed extra room in the shoe to accommodate the painful bunion.

Shoe Shaper and Stretcher

Simple lasts, when put into a shoe or boot, ensure its shape or make the shoe more comfortable by stretching it. When heavy leather footwear was the rage, a must have item to prevent agonising pinching.

Digging Boot

Another Victorian device that looks straight out of a horror movie. The idea was that it was strapped to the normal boot. The steel blade then fit into a lip in the top of the spade. It was meant to allow the digger to push down harder onto the spade and reduce wear on the boot. Sounds like jolly hard work and it looks extraordinarily uncomfortable.

More a case of hard labour than labour-saving!

These Boots Are Made for Walking . . .

Boot Protectors

Also known as segs, boot protectors are metal pieces hammered into the heels and tips of the soles. When good leather boots were essential for work and expensive, these segs saved their price many times over—an essential item for all members of the family.

Portable Boot Remover

Boot trapped on your foot in the field? No problem, this military boot remover was portable. Only snag was, which bit went where, and how did it work?

Boot Stretcher

Yet another Victorian instrument of torture? No, thankfully only a tight boot felt the full rigours of this machine. By placing this tool into the boot and tightening the screw, the lower angled metal pieces forced out the leather. Looks like it could do some serious lumber. Not so much "tough as old boots" as "tough as new boots."

Boot Remover

What was it about Victorians and the removal of boots? It appears to have been a herculean task. You see modern versions for decoration cast as beetles, but this one is fully adjustable—just mind it doesn't bite back!

Horning In

Cyclist Shoe Horn

Shoe horns have even been made for certain groups of people. This clever little example is a lightweight horn for bikers, with the added feature of a lace hook enabling boots to be tied quickly and efficiently. Late Victorian.

Advertising Shoe Horn

The interest in this shoehorn is the engraved printing on its surface advertising the "Public Benefit Shoe Company," a manufacturer of shoes and boots. It also has an engraving of a horse and cart carrying a large shoe. A nice gimmick to promote their product.

Comb Hair Cutter

Back in the 1950s, there was a spate of inventions that claimed to save people money by allowing them to cut their own hair. We believe this apparatus predates them and is from the 1930s. As you comb the blade cuts your hair to shape, or at least that's the idea. We wonder whether a pudding basin and a pair of scissors might not have been more effective.

Comb Cleaner Strop

Made with a beautiful silk-like material, a clear swipe through its strands cleaned all the dandruff and anything else, living or dead, that might be in one's locks and tresses. Both clever and useful.

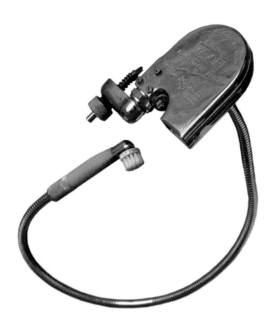

Smile, Please!

Hydraulic Power Toothbrush

The modern electric toothbrush had its predecessor. This well-engineered if unusual 1930s invention used the pressure of water to rotate the brush head. It works really well, but there are drawbacks: it has to be plumbed in to the mains and it produces a constant stream of water into the mouth, which, whilst refreshing and cleansing, is just a little too much.

Toothpick

Since the sixteenth century, toothpicks have been available in all shapes and sizes. This example is Victorian, with the business end able to be folded back into the shaft. Very neat and easy to extract at table.

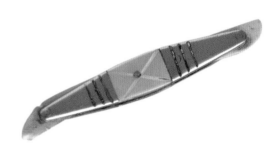

Toothpaste Squeezer, 1950s

To get the very last drop from your tube place it in the serrated teeth and turn the handle. It works, but why not just squeeze with your fingers, and would you ever recoup the cost of the gadget?

Hang On!

Victorian Tree Hanger

We believe the original intention of this hanger was for those out ice skating in the winter to hang their hats whilst on the ice. The gadget opens up and the sharp point fits into the tree, leaving the hook for the hat. It even has a place for a name tag in place of Farrand's of Seaforth, near Liverpool. A handy device for the late-Victorian freezing winters, when rivers and lakes regularly froze over.

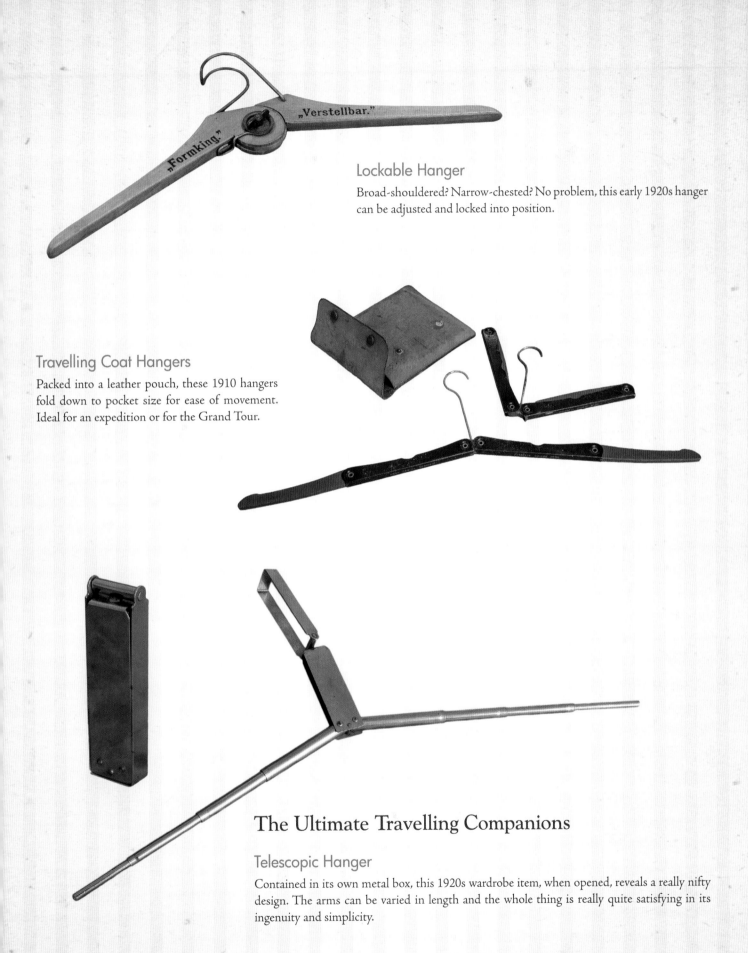

Lockable Hanger

Broad-shouldered? Narrow-chested? No problem, this early 1920s hanger can be adjusted and locked into position.

Travelling Coat Hangers

Packed into a leather pouch, these 1910 hangers fold down to pocket size for ease of movement. Ideal for an expedition or for the Grand Tour.

The Ultimate Travelling Companions

Telescopic Hanger

Contained in its own metal box, this 1920s wardrobe item, when opened, reveals a really nifty design. The arms can be varied in length and the whole thing is really quite satisfying in its ingenuity and simplicity.

Expandable Hanger

Made in a lattice style, this hanging clothes keeper expands, allowing a range of different clothing to be hung on the small metal rings, such as skirts, blouses, etc. Probably from the 1930s.

Collars and Cuffs

All-Purpose Tailor's Measure

This apparatus performed a multitude of measuring tasks, from collars to sleeves.

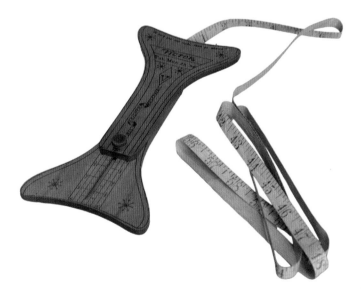

Collar Shaper

This nifty wooden and black plastic gadget shaped the stiff celluloid collar to fit the neck. Simple but effective.

The Collapsing Comb

Opening Comb

Housed in its own wallet, this comb folds down to a third of its original size, making it ideal for the back pocket. Of course, any pickpocket, thinking they had just liberated your hard-earned pound notes, would only be able to tidy their hair!

Press-Button Comb

Housed in a flashy nickel-plated case, a slide of the top knob releases the comb ready for use by the Edwardian gent.

The Business Has Folded!

Sandwich Box

Genuinely innovative. After consuming your sandwiches at lunchtime, the box folds down to a slim, easy-to-handle metal flat container that is much handier to carry back home —brilliant!

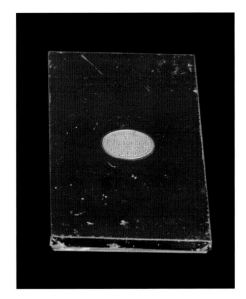

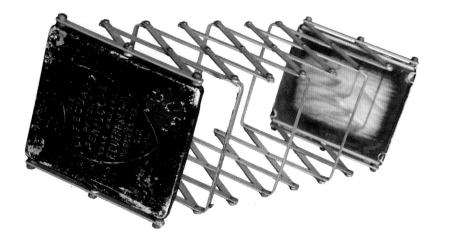

Folding Periscope

Made in Manchester in the early nineteenth century, we believe this was made to see over crowds at pageants or spectacles. Ideal for Victoria's Jubilees later in the century.

Folding Spoon

No need to miss out on the soup! The two handles fold back onto the business end of this piece of cutlery, making it much easier to carry around from function to function. Then again, you would think any self-respecting hotel or restaurant would provide you with spoons!

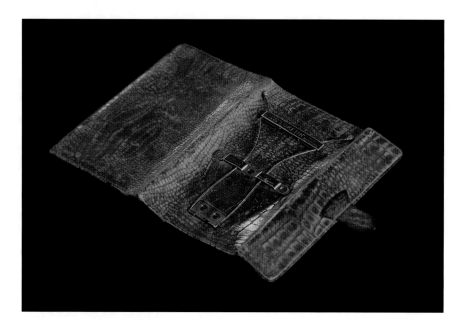

Lockable Wallet

The use of this 1920s leather wallet remains a bit of a mystery. The lock seems just to hold the wallet tight, maybe to keep your notes flat or to stop catching the edges on the side of one's back pocket. It works by simply pulling down the top slide which tightens the springs, thus compressing the wallet. The wallet, however, remains as likely to be pinched as before, and the lock would not stop a determined thief from getting at the pound notes. Does a reader have any further information?

Brushing Up on Your Fashion

Brush and Hanger

Can be used as a clothes brush and then used to hang the garment. Natty!

Comfy Strips

Thin bra straps could cut into the shoulders terribly. One answer, apart from a better designed bra strap, were these transparent strips on the shoulder. A bit of a nuisance to fit every time, but a godsend to many.

Hoopla Skirt Structure

In the early '50s the flared skirt was all the rage. But how to get the look? This framework underneath the skirt gave the effect the fashion gurus demanded. In some ways a throwback to the elaborate dress of mid-Victorian ladies, many might have been glad when this fad proved to be short-lived.

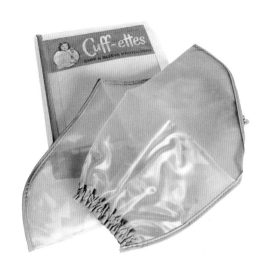

Cuff Protectors

How to keep the sleeves dry and clean when washing up or doing the housework? Here is one answer from an inventor. Something tells me these Cuff-ettes were not a success, and I can hear my mother say a better and cheaper answer was to "roll your sleeves up!"

Strapped to the Wrist

Magnetic Pin Holder

The Victorian seamstress could work with much greater efficiency with this natty gadget fixed to her wrist. The pins adhered to the face of the magnet, allowing the dressmaker to turn up the skirt or fix a hem. Alternatively, if bored with her work she could carry out experiments in ferromagnetics or devise a simple compass!

Motorists Note Pad

With motor cars in the 1920s came gadgets for the motorist. Need to jot something down whilst bowling along in your jalloppy? Just scribble the note onto the paper in this clever wrist pad. Need more room? Just move the paper on with the little winders. Hang on, have you still got hold of the steering wheel? Crikey! Perhaps not such a good idea after all!

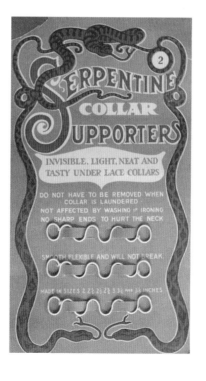

Fob Watch Adaptor

In Victorian times, fob watches were the norm for men and women, but the soldiers during WWI preferred wristwatches, a fashion brought across from America. In the 1920s, wristbands like these were developed to allow small fob watches to be worn on the wrist. Doesn't look particularly comfortable, though.

Getting Collared

Collar Stays

Three of these simple Edwardian gadgets are still affixed to one of the display cards. Their job was to keep the collar in perfect shape around the neck—I always wondered how that was done.

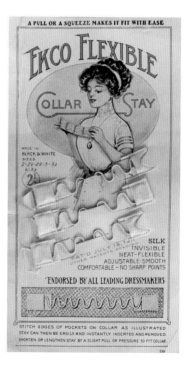

Ruff and Collar Iron

A Victorian collar and sleeve ruff iron that would shape pleats into the fashion of the period.

Walking on Ice

Ice and Mud Walkers

The idea of these overshoes was to keep your best footwear away from the muck and the slush, but the rings on the bottom look lethal on ice and a sure thing for a broken bone or two.

Ice Crampons

The intrepid Victorian climber would wear these crampons climbing the Alps. They do give the most amazing grip.

Ice Creepers

Similar devices are still sold today; they strap onto the shoe to give extra grip on icy pavement.

Prolonging the Life of Shoes

Blakey's Segs—manufactured for many years by Pennine Castings Ltd of Leeds but now owned by H. Goodwin Castings—started life as "Blakey Shoe Segs and Protectors" in 1902, originally concentrating on shoes rather than boots. Prior to this, in 1880, Mr. John Blakey, a prolific inventor who had designed many types of novel innovations mainly connected with shoe machinery, came up with the idea of hammering protective pieces of metal into the soles of shoes.

These shoe protectors continue to be a niche product in a fiercely competitive market and are still made in the same foundry in Armley, Leeds, as they have been for over a hundred years.

Segs Shoe Studs

The innovation of putting steel plates on the bottom of shoes and boots really had a major impact on the life of footwear. It's great to see the longevity of such a simple idea. These samples are possibly from the late 1940s, and the illustrations of ladies' nylons show even the most dainty of shoes can have a longer life.

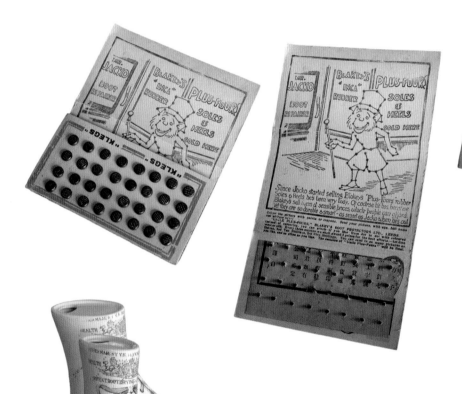

Boots Warm and Dry and Fit for a Queen

Boot Warmers

These lovely boot warming lasts have survived for a century and a half. Still in perfect condition, they are ready to be filled with hot water to warm the boots of the young Queen Victoria—a very different vision of Victoria from the image we have of an old, dour monarch. Quite delightful!

THE DREADED WEED

Ale, gin, wine, and even laudanum may have been addictive to many in Georgian and Victorian Britain, but no addiction was as widespread as that of tobacco. From snuff to cigars, from pipes to fags, people of all classes—men and, increasingly, women—were desperate for another puff or another blast of nicotine. In the first half of the twentieth century this addiction reached epidemic proportions.

There were, and still are, many reasons why smoking was taken up. Some of it was peer pressure, some blatant advertising, but for some it was a prop for tired or miserable lives, something to turn to in times of trouble.

No aspect of smoking was left untouched by gadgets of every kind. Some were to do with the very obvious needs of storing and lighting cigars or cigarettes. Others tried to make chic drawing on a fag. At a time when nearly every movie star had a cigarette to their lips, this was relatively easy to do.

So, whether you are or have been an inhaler on the dreaded weed, or whether you have steered clear of this addiction, here is the story of the great tobacco craze told through gadgets and gizmos.

Gadgets Worthy of 007

In real life, Ian Fleming smoked exclusive cigarettes from Morland's of Grosvenor Street. In "real" life James Bond smoked the same Macedonian blend. Both these novelty gadgets could be from the "real" world of spies, microfilms, and dead letter drops.

Collapsible Pipe

This novelty item shaped like a bottle turns into a pipe by just unscrewing the base from the neck. By screwing the two parts together it becomes a smoke-able pipe, or else it contains the microfilm.

Pistol Lighter and Cigarette Case

This life-like pistol was not only a container for tobacco but also a lighter; you just pulled the trigger. By the way, did I mention . . .the name's Bond, James Bond.

Shaping the Cigar

Cigar Cutter

A very unusual Edwardian cutter that mechanises cigar smoking and, you would think, takes some of the preparatory pleasure from the act.

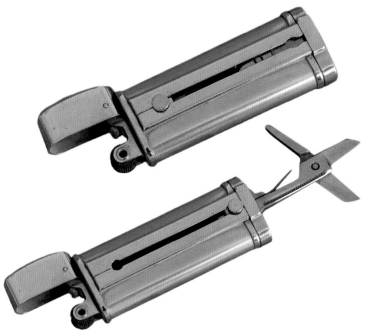

Cigar Lighter, Cutter, and Pricker

This wonderfully neat, all-in-one pocket tool from the 1920s is like the cigar smoker's Swiss Army knife: one quick flick and all the tools you need before lighting up are there.

Cigar-Shaped Flute

An Edwardian novelty—I can't believe it had a serious purpose. Who said gimmicks were new-fangled?

Some "Baccy" Ideas

Intercahangeable Pipe Barrels

A novel idea to allow the pipe smoker to choose the barrel for look as well as taste. Each barrel has the ability to be screwed into the pipe stem—a clever idea from Edwardian times.

Cigarette Ashtray and Holder

From the 1920s, this combination ashtray and holder attempted to solve the problem of not wishing to finish a cigarette at one go. Apparently, you would stick your fag upright on one of the spikes and then return to take another drag in a few minutes. We believe the centre compartment was for matches.

Cigar Box and Lock

This lovely cigar box with its attachment of lock and matches would have been used in the dining rooms of stately homes in the 1920s. We think the idea of the lock was to ensure the servants didn't snaffle the odd smoke!

Light Up Automatically

Metal Striker

Inside the metal striker is a small wick infused with a small amount of lighter fluid. This striker is pulled hard against the serrated side of the gadget, creating sparks that light the wick. It also has a pipe bowl cleaner and a damper as accessories. Then again, why not just buy an ordinary lighter?

Automatic Match Striker

This canny Edwardian invention lights a match that has dropped into place from the tiny silo. A hard push on the metal pin forces the match head against the metal striker and it bursts into flame. Seems a little elaborate—why not just an ordinary matchbox?

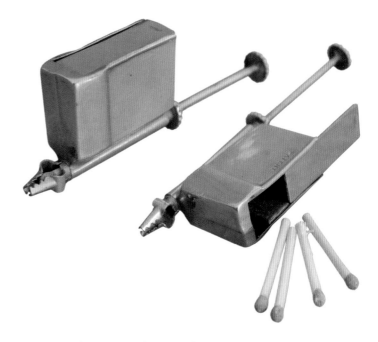

Faggish Paraphernalia

Telescopic Ladies' Cigarette Holder

Very neat patent allowing it be stored away in a lady's bag, though lacking the chic look—perhaps not to be used during breakfast at Tiffany's!

Cigarette Ashtray with Self-Striking Matches

Just by pulling out a single red strand from the circle of matches immediately causes it to flare. From around the 1920s. But with all that hot fag ash in the middle, it's a wonder the whole thing didn't go up!

1930s Cigarette Lighter

You pull out and press down the central nob and a dynamo generates just enough electricity to heat an element at the other end, from which your tobacco can be lit. Similar to a car lighter.

Cigarette Making Machine

So many people rolled their own that there was a plethora of gadgets to help make your own cigarettes. This one is from the 1920s.

Fans of Cigars and Fans from Cigars

Cigar-Shaped Fan Container

Disguising small fans by hiding them in other objects was a trick repeated by the novelty trade many times. They came as pencils, pens, Stanhopes (miniature photograph viewers) and, as in this case, cigars. Made in Japan, 1950s.

Trick Cigar Cutter

Gadgets patented to attend to the needs of smokers abounded, especially in Edwardian times. They came in all shapes and sizes. Here you have a trick cutter that can also be used as a key ring. I doubt the owner of the trick cutter would himself have been "bashful"; rather, one sees him as a rakish fellow and man-about-town!

Cigar-Shaped Lighter

Trick Cigar Cutter

Gadgets patented to attend to the needs of smokers abounded, especially in Edwardian times. They came in all shapes and sizes. Here you have a trick cutter that can also be used as a key ring. I doubt the owner of the trick cutter would himself have been "bashful"; rather, one sees him as a rakish fellow and man-about-town!

When Smoking Was Fashionable

It seemed that everybody did it—from movie stars to ladies of fashion, rich and poor, men and women—smoking was completely socially acceptable. Long before the health warnings from the doctors and long before the unmarked cigarette packets, every conceivable device was invented to tap into this huge market.

Double Cigarette Holder

Sheer madness! Who would ever have thought up such a product, and did it have any success? It seems a tad tawdry despite the fashionable mouthpiece.

Lighter and Case

These combined cigarette cases were the commonest device to fuel the smoking craze. Often very stylish, they added to the chic of smoking.

Little Finger Cigarette Holder

No nicotine-stained fingers for the lady of fashion; the ring of this holder slipped over a finger. One put one's fag to one's mouth rather as one raised one's little finger whilst sipping one's tea.

Automatic Cigarette Snuffer

This gadget automatically turned over the butt and put it out in one go. Notice the stylish oyster shell ashtray—everything to make a fundamentally messy and dangerous habit appealing to all classes.

Vaping for the Victorians

Cigarette Perfumer

It is rare one comes across a more unusual item than this cigarette injecting needle. It does what it says on the box: itself a lovely reminder of good Victorian design. The needle injects the perfume of your choice into the cigarette, giving you the aroma you want or the one most suited to your personality! The apparatus undoes to give access to a phial into which you put the perfume, the cigarette is placed into the end, and you press the plunger. Very similar to the present day e-cigarette, which runs nearly fifty different scents and flavours.

LEISURE TIME AND KEEPING FIT

Automation, mechanisation, and gadgetry of every kind were meant to free us for hour after hour of leisure and pleasure. We all say that lives, far from becoming more relaxed, have become ever more frenetic, yet the range of opportunities for sport, entertainment, and having a good time have expanded enormously. And with more leisure pursuits come more gizmos and contraptions.

Going to the gym may be a modern craze, but many have been trying to keep fit for years. Here there are massagers and body strengtheners going back as far as Victorian times.

Organised sport needed technology, whether to keep the net at the right height in tennis or to improve at golf. Many well known firms became involved in the manufacture of sports equipment.

Gambling, in all its forms, saw gadgets to fleece the unwary. There were mechanical card dealers for the serious player, as well as early versions of the lottery. If you could pull yourself away from the card table, you could always go on a shoot and bag a few grouse.

A Bit of Fun or a Mug's Game?

Give-Away Portrait Maker

A clever advertising gimmick: the face is made up of a thin wire chain. You tap the card to make a face. As it says in the ditty, it will bring a smile to the face, especially if you have used Mazo tablets to clean your clothes. Rather sweet.

Pools Line Maker

Before the lottery there were football (soccer) pools. Here you shake the box to get a predicted line. Saves worrying about the actual teams. By the look of it, the box may predict too many away wins.

Horse Racing Roulette

Now this really is a mug's game, but this beautifully crafted roulette wheel would while away the hours and lose you loads of dosh. Place your bets, spin the wheel, and hope it's your nag that stops at the winning post. Go on, give me some odds on winning . . .

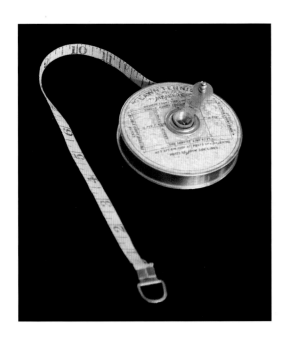

A Good Sport

Tennis Court Measure

Inventions around pastimes were just as common as those for more mundane purposes. As leisure time gradually increased, so did the range of gadgets aimed at sports and amusements.

Ladies' Tennis Hair Net

Automatic Billiard Ball Dispenser

Clever: the table is three balls short—a red and two yellows. Drop your money in and the flap opens—game on!

Flicker Football Book

Within living memory, these flicker picture books entranced children with "moving" pictures. Try telling that to young people nowadays . . .

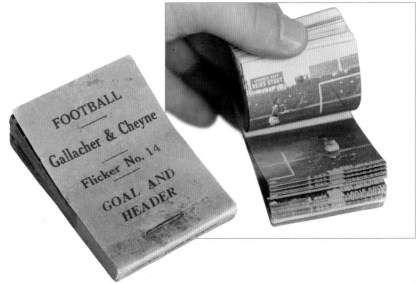

Deal or No Deal?

Lone Arm Card Holder

It won't be a surprise that this was produced in WWI to allow many soldiers who had lost an arm fighting in the trenches to be able to occupy themselves in hospitals and homes by playing cards.

Automatic Card Dealer

Made in the 1920s, a twirl of the lever gives out four hands of cards, one at a time. There have been many mechanical card dealers in production since then, but this is one of the originals.

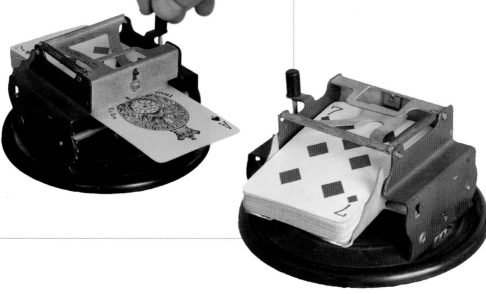

Cardsharp Gadget

The story goes this product holds the cards of the "sharp" whilst playing a hand. When needed, the trump card is delivered from the sleeve held by the gadget to the table.

The "Square Dealer"

Card Dealer

No need to wait for a possibly unscrupulous dealer to laboriously give out four hands at the table. Though looking a trifle too mechanical and possibly inelegant for the card table of a club or a casino, this 1907 "Square Dealer" is certainly a well-engineered machine. A speedy way to hasten the winning or losing of money.

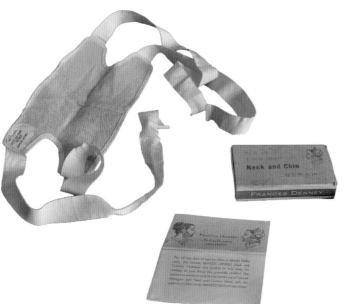

Chest, Arms, and Chin

Double Chin Remover

Sadly, another quack item to deceive Edwardian ladies into believing there was an easy answer to the inevitable ravages of time.

Victorian Water Wings

We've tried them and they work! Indeed, you would nearly take off from the water given how much "lift" around your arms and neck these water wings produce when inflated.

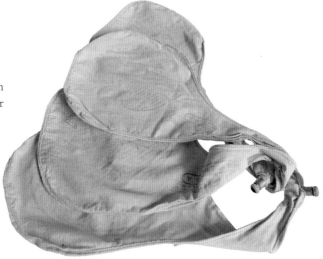

Protective Jacket

A bit of a mystery this one. Is it for keeping the cold out? Or is it medicated in some way? We are not sure of its use —can you help?

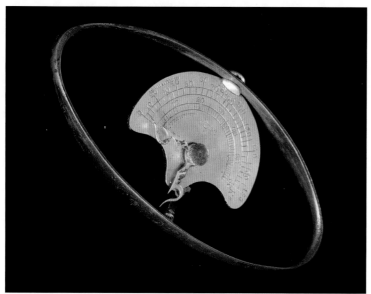

Handholding

Hand Strength Indicator

With this 1910 muscle developer you can see progress every day. Every time you exercise the pointer swivels around the scale to demonstrate your ever-improving physique.

Hand Strengthener

A simple exercise machine from the early part of the twentieth century. Gives the muscles in the hands a good workout. The tension in the springs resists each pull. Gives you a vice-like handshake—it really works!

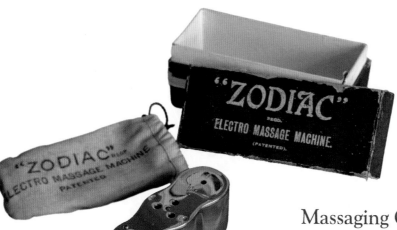

Massaging One's Ills Away

Electro Massager

Made in the 1940s, the movement of the massaging wheel turned a magneto—a dynamo with fixed magnets—to produce an added electric shock.

Back Massager

Holding the two handles, those in need of a hard blood surfacing massage would place the contraption across the back and pull to and fro. The wooden balls do the trick. Around 1910.

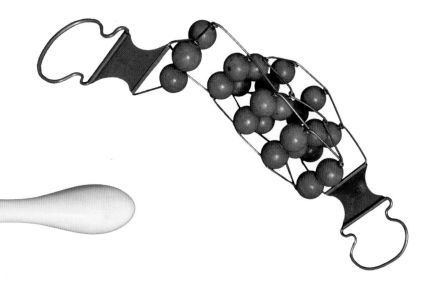

Body Massager

Probably manufactured in the 1930s, this massager could be used anywhere on the body. The concentration of plastic balls would give a very deep massage.

"Not with My Back the Way It Is . . ."

These early physiotherapy tools are skillfully designed and wonderfully crafted. They are utilitarian, yet very attractive.

Vibrating Back Massager

Made in the 1920s, this beautifully designed contraption not only pounds the flesh, but could also vibrate at the same time. The masseur or physiotherapist just has to keep winding hard—good for the therapist and the patient.

Rubber Based Massager

This is a simple massaging contraption. Its therapeutic effect comes from the rubber plug-like attachments on the roller. Running it over your body and applying some pressure at the same time causes extra blood to flow, lessening muscle pain.

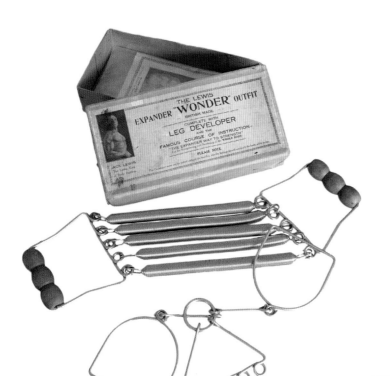

Exercise — Muscles and Bowls

Leg Developers

In the past as today, some men have worried about being the thin emaciated lad on the beach having sand flicked into their face. Worry no more! Throughout the 1930s home body developers such as this abounded.

Advertising Bowls Measure

Since the object of a game of bowls is to get closer to the jack than your opponent, it's essential to be able to accurately measure the distance between jack and bowls to decide who has won. In an official match it would be the umpire doing the measuring, but for informal practise games you'll want your own measuring accessories handy. Capstan cigarettes saw another advertising opportunity and produced this give-away for use on the green.

Let's Get Physical

Leg Exercisers

Place your foot in the stirrup, grasp the other end, and pull! Great for strengthening leg and arm muscles.

Dumbbells

These clever dual-function dumbbells not only allow you to do weight exercises, but also strengthen your grip.

Tennis Ball Cleaner

For those not fortunate enough to be playing on the immaculate surfaces at Wimbledon, just drop dirty tennis balls into the aperture at the top of the machine, give a quick turn of the handle, and the brushes inside remove the dirt, then you're ready for the next serve.

Supporting the Ankle

Ankle Support

Patented in the late Victorian period, below is an extract from the actual patent:

Introduced into an ordinary shoe and to act to strengthen or sustain the ankle, in order that the ankle may not bend inwardly or outwardly under the weight of the person, and this device is especially adapted to children with weak ankles, but it may also be used for T supporting ankles in those more advanced in age. In the ankle supporters heretofore constructed the side portions have been united to a greater or lesser extent at the back of the heel, and in consequence thereof several difficulties have been encountered.

Such difficulties are evidently overcome with this leather strapping for the ankle.

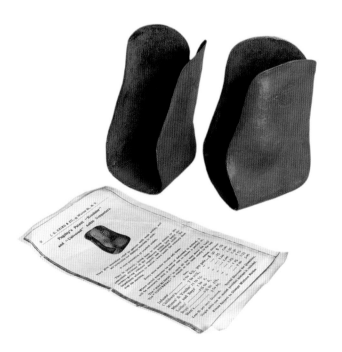

Metal and Leather Carrier

Playing the Game

Game Carriers

The British aristocracy loved their annual shoot. Every season off would go the squires with their shooting party, the idea being to bag as much game as possible in a day. The pheasants and grouse—birds raised and guarded over the year by gamekeepers—were flushed out by beaters, ready for the hunters to shoot down.

Each of these carriers was designed for a different "bag." The heads of the poor birds were placed in the slots provided on the carrier—they allowed for a sizeable haul.

Leather Thonged Carrier

Wooden Double Carrier

Duck or Grouse

Clay Pigeon Shooter

Spring actuated skeet throwers are excellent tools for sportsmen because they throw clay pigeons (skeets) accurately every time and one person can operate the machine. Vintage skeet throwers such as this are solid steel and feature stands, long throwing arms, hands to hold the clay pigeons, and a rope. The machine is set up by loading it with the skeet and pulling back the arm until it latches. The sportsman then pulls the rope to throw the pigeon. This example is from the early twentieth century.

Duck Caller

Another device for the sportsman, this time for shooting real birds. This elaborate looking concertina-type caller makes a really loud quack. By pumping the rubber coils it emits a remarkably accurate duck noise.

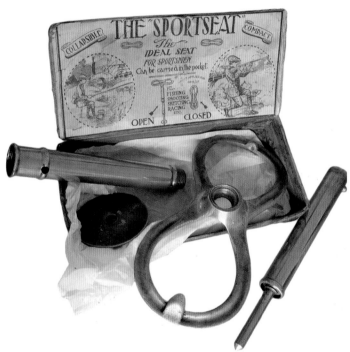

A Place for the Posterior

Collapsible Shooting Stick

Packed into its own tin container sized to go into the pocket and produced to help the gentry enjoy their hunting, shooting, and fishing.

Wonderfully engineered, allowing the seat to be snapped together in seconds.

Cleaning Up at Golf

Golf Ball Cleaner

Like a miniature hot water bottle, the rubber golf ball cleaner was patented in 1922 and remained in use for over twenty years. Here was a successful invention. It allowed two golf balls to be cleaned simultaneously by swirling about in the water. Ingenious and simple.

Golf Scorer

Manufactured in the '20s, this enabled the player to keep his/her score mechanically, rather than by using pencil and paper. Presumably you would still have to fill out a club scorecard before reaching the nineteenth hole?

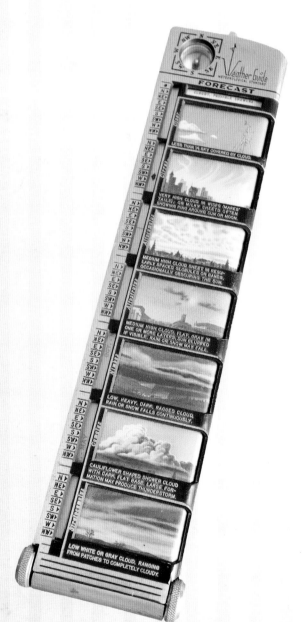

Anyone for Tennis?

Weather Forecaster

You look at the sky, fit the picture to those on the contraption, and the future weather is forecast.

An amazingly expensive product for something so easy to check oneself.

Tennis Pole

If the weather is set fair, set up the net for tennis with this finely engineered early Edwardian pole.

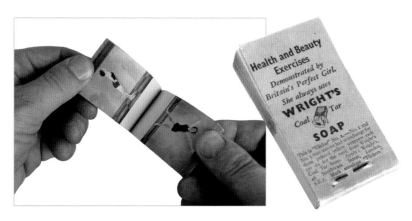

Get Fit Flicker Book

Even if the weather isn't fit for tennis, you can always get fit yourself by exercising. Then again, you can always just flick the pages and watch Britain's perfect girl do them instead.

A clever marketing device for Wright's Coal Tar soap.

It's Just Not Cricket, It's Golf

Captive Golf Ball

At least you won't lose this one in the rough!

"Owzthat" Cricket Game

How many generations of youngsters have enjoyed the simple pleasures of this miniature game of dice? What centuries have been scored, what tests have been won with this pocket-sized gem over the years?

Cricket Bat String Winder

Before rubber padding, the handles of cricket bats were often covered with a special string-like material woven around and around to absorb the shock of the bat meeting the ball. This beautifully crafted device dates from the 1920s; only snag is, it has us foxed. We haven't quite been able to work out how it works—perhaps one of the readers of this book may be able to enlighten us!

Novelty Entertainment

The use of novelties to promote company brands has long been a feature of the marketing of goods, at least until the advent of the Internet. Normal products, such as small toys, would be turned into promotional give-aways to give greater and longer-lasting exposure of their name, whether it was Wills's Woodbines with their dominoes or Dunn & Co, who, you will note, had branches everywhere.

Table Bowls

The game played on the green turned into a home table game: same rules, but in miniature.

Dominoes

One of the very oldest pub games, dominoes would have a use wherever people gathered. In WWI, games such as this would have been sent to soldiers in the trenches to occupy their time whilst waiting to go "over the top."

Kiss Flicker Book

By flicking the book with your finger, the story of "The Kiss" is told in cinematic style.

Tricks with Sticks

Inside the matchbox container are sticks and a leaflet showing a range of tricks you can do to amaze your friends, all the while giving the company maximum exposure.

From Boy Scouts to Gamblers and Drinkers

Trick Snuff Box

"OPEN THE BOX AND WE WILL STAND YOU A JOHNNIE WALKER."

Used by the whisky company Johnnie Walker as a give-away. The idea was the man behind the bar would bet that if the punter could open the box and take his bit of snuff he would get a free whisky. I know how to do it, do you?

Gaming Watch

Used by the totally hooked gambler, this watch would suggest odds on which to bet. With the night well on and the brain well gone, this device can be brought out from the pocket and the "on the spot casino" would then be in full swing.

Sunwatch Compass

This 1930s device was sold to Boy Scouts. It could be used by them to get their topographical badge. Of course, the ordinary traveller could use it as well whilst rambling on the moors. However, beware, if there is a fog or low cloud you will get lost. Better pack an ordinary magnetic compass!

Cricket Ball Gauge

It's Not Cricket!

If a cricket ball goes out of shape it gives an unfair advantage to the bowling side. Here is the answer. If the ball cannot pass through the maximum diameter, passes through the minimum diameter, or becomes misshapen, the umpires should replace the ball. The replacement ball is ideally an old ball that was used in a previous match for a comparable number of overs as the ball being replaced, so it has had approximately the same amount of use and wear as the old ball—once again to keep things fair and ensure it *is* cricket!

This gauge is probably Edwardian.

Craps, Dice-Less

Give-Away Craps Gambler

7 = 11 (craps) is a dice game in which players make bets on the outcome of the roll, or a series of rolls, of a pair of dice. Players may wager money against each other (playing "street craps," also known as "shooting dice" or "rolling dice"). Because it requires little equipment, "street craps" can be played nearly anywhere. This advertising give-away makes it even easier to play craps—and lose your money —by doing away with the dice altogether. Just a twirl of the promotional toy puts the small ball into a numbered slot, roulette style. The reverse is the advertisement. I just love the young lady's eyes—she's watching you!

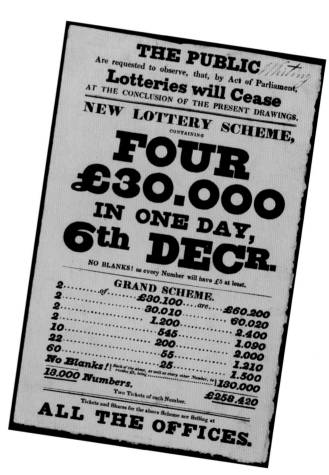

Lottery Flyer

So, the National Lottery is a new thing? Not a bit of it. Cash-strapped British governments have regularly played on our gambling instincts to help fund wars or swell the coffers. Elizabeth I had one, and the English State Lottery ran from 1694 until 1826. We believe this handbill is from the latter year. It was issued by stockbrokers T. Bish & Co. from their offices at 4 Cornhill and 9 Charing Cross. How many hopes over those 132 years will have been pinned on those lucky numbers?

Gambling Machine

This 1930s gadget is a roulette wheel for the home or the party. Give it a spin, and what are the chances of you losing your stake, if not the shirt off your back?

GADGETS FOR ALL

Which came first, the chicken or the egg? Did the inventor spot a need and use all his ingenuity to meet that need, or did he, purely for the joy of creating or, perhaps more likely, to pay the rent, come up with some crazy contraption that never quite met anybody's needs? Few of the inventors in this book will have been so altruistic as to design a better mouse trap just for the joy of it and the pleasure it would bring to the mouse-infested householder. Nearly every engineer, manufacturer, and Heath-Robinson in this book will have thought their next idea would be the next big thing, and, consequently, bring riches and reward.

Some made it, like the carpet-laying grippers that became tools of the trade. Some did not, like the "home haircutter." Then there are those gadgets that presage our own clever devices, such as the dynamo torch and pistol torch, the essentials of which can be found in the wind-up torches of today.

Every one of these gadgets would take hours of designing, making, testing, and manufacturing. They may all delight us today, even if some of them never quite made it with the public.

So here they are: something for everyone and a miscellany of gadgets, gizmos, and contraptions for your amazement and delectation!

Made to Fit Everyone's Pocket

Pocket Rotoscope

An Edwardian three-dimensional pocket viewer.

Throwaway Pocket Spittoon

Inside the package is a small cardboard box: you spit, then throw away the whole lot, spit and all.

Pocket Door Wedge

What's so neat is the wooden insert that opens this Victorian gadget to just the right angle to wedge the door securely —but why would you want to carry a door wedge round with you?

Pocket Glass Spittoon

You remove any unwanted phlegm from your mouth into the large opening of the jar, then, when at home, you wash the whole thing out through the bottom hole.

Rubber-Dub-Dub

Adhesive Plaster

The plaster we use today to cover our cuts and bruises had its forerunner, but in full sheets that needed cutting to the size required. From the Edwardian period, these type of plasters began a major industry that exists till today, yet the question remains, why are there always so many large plasters and not enough of the little ones in the assorted packs of today?

Rubber Stamp

Looking like a fob watch with the chain ready to be affixed to the belt of the Victorian gentleman, it was a quick and easy way to stamp one's name and address when required on documents and letters. Victorian gents loved things on fobs and chains: their very trousers and waistcoats must have been burdened down by watches and gadgets of all descriptions.

Phone Cap

The rubber ring has been impregnated with deodoriser and possibly some germ killing agent. The interesting copy indicates its use in a public phone box, when private phone lines were still a rarity.

Warming the Bed and Belly

Bed Warmer

Essentially a firebrick, the bed warmer was heated up in the glowing embers of the fire in the evening, then carried by the maid to one's bed. How was it carried? And mind your toes on it once in bed in case you burn yourself!

Belly Warmer

This is the daddy of all belly warmers! We believe it may have been used by the more portly Victorian male, but it could also have been for horses with a bad stomach. Made of ceramic and really very heavy.

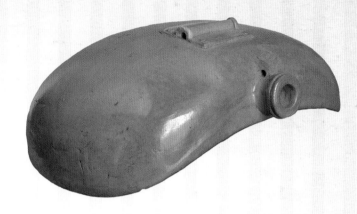

Belly Warmer

A lovely tin warmer possibly used by early Victorian coachmen when they needed to be out and about on a cold winter morning. It straps around the body above the vest and below the shirt.

Getting into Hot Water

Muff Warmer

The hot water bottle for the lady in the carriage. It would be wrapped in her muff round her hands and arms to keep off the chill of bitter cold Victorian winters.

Electric Hot Water Bottle

In the '30s, the use of plastic and the development of electricity created the opportunity to warm your bed by plugging in this replacement "hot water bottle." The precursor to the electric blanket.

Heated Hair Curler

Looking more like an instrument of torture, this simple 1920s curler worked by filling it with boiling water and then twisting it like a brush through hair. No wonder electric tongs and hair curlers took off!

Triggering Light in the Darkness

Dynamo Torch

Long before today's wind-up radios and torches, dynamos were used to power torches without batteries. In this case, you just pulled the ring at the base of the torch to give a light that lasted up to two minutes. Probably produced in WWII. Worn round the neck. There is a snag, though: it is very heavy, but then again, virtually indestructible.

Gun Torch

Possibly a toy torch, although it could have been a novel way of lighting one's way in the dark, giving a certain amount of confidence and courage. Made in the 1930s.

The Paper Trail

Automatic Blotter

In the days of genuine ink pens, blotting paper always needed to be at hand to soak up excess ink.

This device may seem a little over the top for the scale of the problem. Blotting paper was attached to the arm and, when you gave the knob a push, it turned round over the top of the document.

Paper Drinking Cup

We think throw away paper cups are a modern invention, but here is an American cup from about 1912, proving they were in use much earlier. Billy Arlington as "The Laughing Hobo" was a comic act of the times.

Advertising Paper Weight

Paper weights were often given away in the late nineteenth and early twentieth centuries by companies to promote their wares. This lovingly designed label for Johnsons wax is a really good example of early graphics—you can see the shine on the table!

Sounding Off

Metropolitan Police Whistle

It's unusual to find an original police whistle from London. We believe this one dates from the 1920s.

Penny Clacker

These would have been sold outside Victorian theatres—mainly music halls—and if you didn't like the act, a swift turn on the handle caused a horrendous noise. And we think modern audiences are noisy and rude!

Bird Call

There are many different bird calls, each for a different species. Sadly, I have forgotten the particular bird this caller attracts, but one turn of the small handle gets it flying.

Bicycle Hooter

We believe this to be an Edwardian hooter. It has a squawker box that when pressed gives out a fair old hoot. More effective and certainly more quaint than a mere bicycle bell.

Go On, Give Us a Whistle

Boy Scout Combined Whistle

Be prepared! Boy Scouts seemed endlessly in danger of getting lost and disorientated and here is one of many solutions. It's obviously a whistle, and the compass stands out as a way to find one's way through the countryside, but what was the little hole in the middle for? Well, it gives the blower the ability to communicate in Morse code—things like SOS and "I am lost!"

Whistling Toothbrush

Not sure the child was meant to be able to clean their teeth and whistle a tune on the brush at the same time, but a great idea for encouraging youngsters at bath time.

Blood's Whistling Kettle

Dating from the 1920s, this unusual kettle for the hot plate or the stove has a simple whistle in the spout—just mind you don't burn yourself on the metal handles!

More Than Just a Pen . . .

Pen Razor

The concept of hiding gadgets and making them look like a pen seems to have taken hold of inventors in the early twentieth century. Here you have an assortment of innovations, from razors that could be carried easily in one's breast pocket to the blotter in the top of a pen. This latter is particularly clever. Every time you made a mistake you just rolled the blotter over the mess, but surely the blotter would soon become saturated with ink, unless you were hardly ever given to error—perhaps a gadget more for the saint than the sinner!

Combined Pen and Pencil

Pen with Blotter

Pencil and Lighter Pen

Ray Of Sunshine

Sollux Ray Machine

In the '30s, it was possible to bask in "tropical sunshine" from these lamps, which were supposed to give a great sense of well being without even setting foot outside the door. They were marketed as legitimate medical therapy for those with muscle aches. Beautifully designed in the era of art deco.

The lamp was practical and easy to transport, and it had a dual function. It was not in fact a U-V lamp, which was probably just as well, as it was not only intended to be therapeutic, but could also be used as a reading lamp by the simple expedient of removing the red filter.

Make a Note of This . . .

Paper Music Mender

A paper-backed mending tape for sheet music and other uses. As with so many Victorian artefacts, the packaging or, in this case, the dispenser are finished to the highest standards.

Car Note Taker

The 1920s saw a rash of these devices; this one attaches to the dashboard. Ingenious—just don't start scribbling whilst you are steering the vehicle!

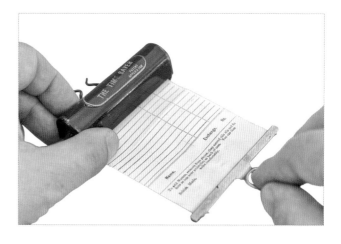

Paper Fasteners

Most legal documents in the nineteenth century would have been held together using these sharp little fasteners.

Pencil with Notepaper

The roll of notepaper is wrapped around the head of the pencil, so how on earth do you write on it?

Small, Portable, and Convenient

Wash-Up Kit

Containing all the requirements whilst away from home. Probably from the 1920s, looking at the man's swimming costume.

Washing Line

All ready to use when out camping or on holiday. Ideal for drying one's undies, it has pegs, cord line, and holder in a neat travelling case. Around the 1930s.

Pocket Heater

Once again, Victorians were obsessed with keeping warm and warding off chills. This example is from America, where it would be even more useful in the depths of winter. This attractive and neat metal-plated charcoal burner fits snugly in your pocket. I can see snags—what if it started to burn through your pocket, what about the possibility of carbon monoxide poisoning, and was there not a serious danger that the seat of your pants might really be on fire?

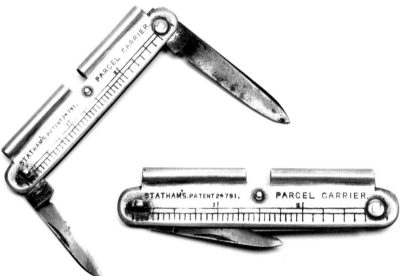

Holders, Carriers, Cutters, and Servers

Knife, Ruler, and Parcel Carrier

A late-Victorian knife that doubles as a ruler, carrier, and of course a string cutter. Ideal for the postie or the dispatch department operative.

Luggage and Book Carrier

A classier—and more expensive—version of classic Victorian carrying handles. The straps fit around a pile of books, suitcase, or box, enabling large weights to be lifted with ease.

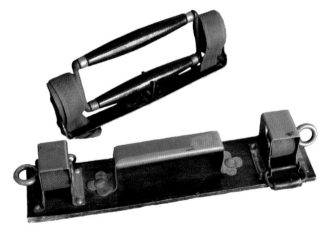

Waiter's Champagne Server

To avoid upsetting those sitting at table having dinner in posh restaurants, this '30s arm extension allowed the bubbly to be poured no matter the position of the glasses on the table. Actually looks a trifle crude and clumsy—a wonder the poor waiter didn't clunk diners' heads with it!

Keeping One's Cool!

Clockwork Fan

A very rare clockwork fan from the Victorian period. The spring is especially large and strong to keep the blades turning longer.

Mechanical Hand Fan

Like a present-day wind-up torch, this clever little gadget from the 1930s just needs a lot of thumb power. Mind you're not all fingers and thumbs, though, as it looks like it could do some serious lumber—then you might not be all fingers and thumbs!

Get Knotted — Making Rope

Scissor Knot Cutter

Unable to unpick the knot? No knot-picker in the drawer? Then just use these specially made scissors that open the parcel with one closure of the blades. Or alternatively, just cut the string with an ordinary pair of scissors. But these are a clever alternative, and the string can be reused!

Rope Maker

To weave cord into a strong rope. Cord is attached to each hook, the handle is turned, and the highly geared machine plaits the rope.

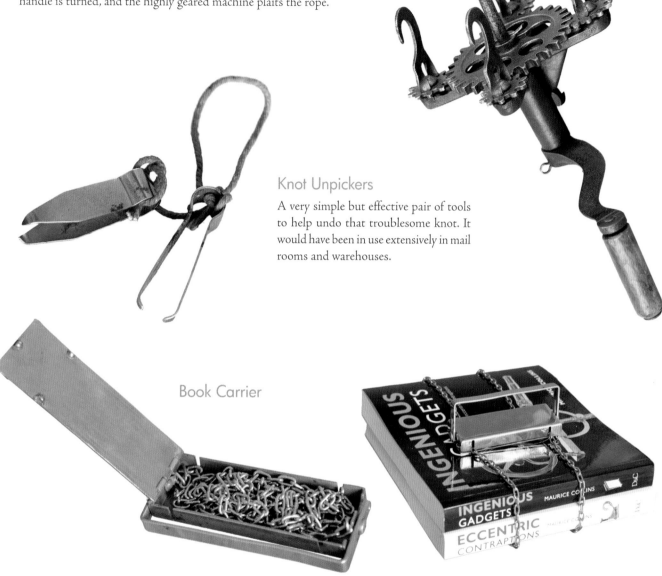

Knot Unpickers

A very simple but effective pair of tools to help undo that troublesome knot. It would have been in use extensively in mail rooms and warehouses.

Book Carrier

More Ingenious Than Eccentric

This clever, handy, and compact book and parcel carrier is a fine example of small inventions of the age.

Having the original advertisement at hand gives all the information needed to understand the uses and cost of this device.

The testimonial from Miss Murray of Ulverston is just wonderful: indeed, it is really so sweet, pretty, and useful a little testimonial that we are quite charmed by Miss Murray.

Just one snag: if one failed to find the centre of gravity of a pile of books or a parcel, the whole lot would come slipping out one end or the other. Even Miss Murray of Ulverston might have found this a trifle annoying.

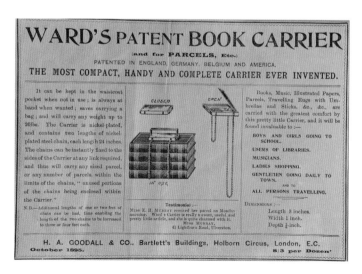

The Readesk

Put that laptop away. Put down the Kindle˚. Forget about e-books. The future is here! Some contraptions are designed to sell well. Others are not. I suspect the Readesk comes under the "not" category. What a wonderfully elaborate solution to a problem that probably hardly existed. Of course, paperback books were still a novelty in the thirties, and if you really wanted to pore over some great leather-bound tome in bed perhaps the Readesk was the answer . . . or maybe "not."

Restful Reading Desk

Patented in the late thirties, the instructions in the leaflet read as follows:

> Pull out the feet as shown above
> Pull out the extension rods
> Adjust the focus by turning the knobs
> Catch the cord behind the small peg on the nob
> Adjust the height of the rest ledge
> If the cord casts a shadow catch it in the notch under the ledge

A complicated system to get comfortable with, but an innovation of its time.

A Type of Printing

Home Printing Kit

Hard to believe that from the sixteenth century printing was produced by a system called letterpress. All books and newspapers were published using moveable type, so the letters could be used over and over again. The type had to be set—a laborious and skilled process. How different things are today with a myriad of fonts and print sizes available at the dab of a finger.

This concept of moveable type is here being used as a home printing kit. This version—"John Bond's" from the 1920s—is essentially the same as the "John Bull" printing kits familiar to children in the 1950s and '60s in the UK. Just as fiddly, yet also just as engrossing.

Our Feathered Friends

Clockwork Bird Caller

This unique caller can repeatedly chant its call by winding the clockwork spring. It keeps going till the spring is unwound. Lovely if it is the sound of a song thrush, but what if the urban householder is in dispute with a neighbour and buys a "Cockerel?"

Pin Dispenser

This lovely flocked box (no pun intended) contains clips of pins for the seamstress to use. By just turning the handle the bird picks up the required metal pin. One has to marvel at the artistic imagination of the inventor. Seamstressing could be a pretty monotonous if skilled job. At least this box and its cheerful yellow canary might brighten up a dull day.

From the Corner Shop to the Drawing Room

Paper Bag Dispenser and Holder

We often think the plastic bag dispensers in our local supermarket must be the latest technology, but back in the '20s, the corner shop had it well organised already.

Automatic Music Sheet Turner

Just place the music score on the stand and press the wooden lever to turn the pages as you play a melodious tune on the piano.

This beautifully constructed music stand demonstrates all the virtuosity of the Victorian and Edwardian inventor. It not only turns the pages, but holds the score open—how often do musicians struggle to turn to and retain the correct page? As so often with sophisticated gadgets of this period, the finish is to a very high standard.

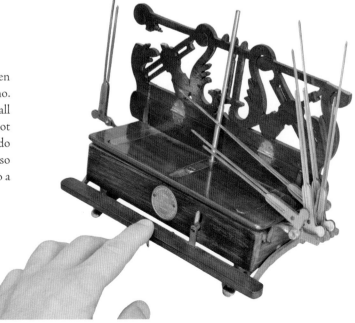

It's a Wind-Up!

What did we do before electricity? How did we cope before every gadget was powered by batteries? Were we in the Stone Age before electric motors, relays, transistors, and microchips operated our every device? No, of course not. The world operated like clockwork. Well, most of the time. Newton and Liebniz may have seen God as the ultimate clock maker, but it was good old physical labour that kept the pre-electronic world ticking along. "Turn, Turn, Turn," as Pete Seeger sung. In fact, the seasons were about the only thing that didn't need muscle power to make them work.

Clockwork Burglar Alarm

Intruders beware! This early 1900s bell would make a heck of a din. Wind it up, place it under the door, and wait for the burglar to push down farther on the lever as he opened the door—Drrrring! Send for the constabulary at once!

Clockwork Coffee Grinder

A beautifully engineered Edwardian machine that grinds your coffee beans into coffee powder, ready for making the very best latte, espresso, Americano, mocha, mélange, cappucino . . . I say, what about opening a coffee bar on every street corner . . . No, the idea would never take off.

Clockwork Fly Catcher

The only action that seems to come from winding up this invention is a slow turning trap in the base to let the fly drop. But why? The poor creature is already held by two gauze nets.

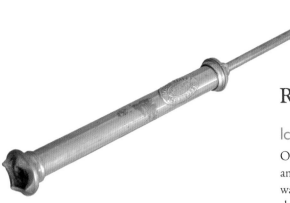

Ready, Aim, Melt!

Ice Breaker

One would need to be very careful when using this artefact. In the days of ice houses and before refrigerators, cutting a block of ice for something as simple as ice in drinks was serious business. This plunger had a sharp steel tip and needed a hard blow to the plunger to split the block of ice.

De-Froster Gun

Just be careful where you point this! This 1950s device was plugged into the cigarette lighter in the dashboard. Not only would it be a huge drain on the battery—especially on a very cold morning, just when it was most difficult to get the engine to turn over—but that sort of direct heat onto the glass of the period would surely have shattered many a windscreen.

Ice Cube Maker and Ice Shoveller

The arrival of the refrigerator from the 1930s on made redundant large blocks of ice in the cellars of larger houses. Now the domestic kitchen could produce ice cubes for cocktails or that cooling drink. This early ice tray froze water in the lower level. When taken out of the refrigerator warm water was added to the top, releasing the ice cubes. The ice shoveller was then used to fill a tumbler ready for use—"with ice?"

Keeping a Steady Beat

Pen Clip

All you need to do is slip the clip over your pen and it will fit neatly into your pocket.

Metronome Tape

This tape measure doubles as a metronome. But why would even a seamstress need both in one device? She could hardly sew hems and play the piano at the same time!

Pocket Gun

Perhaps somewhat surprisingly, handguns appear to have been easily available to the Victorian public. This firearm is just labelled "pocket gun."

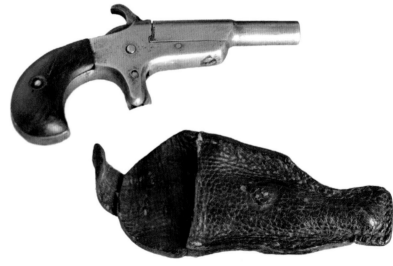

Key Return

Lovely idea prevalent in Edwardian times. If you find the key it tells you to return it to the police. Best of all, "Reward Paid Finder!"

Home Hair Cutter

After television came into the front room this type of gadget was even sold "As Seen on TV," as well as in the sort of direct sales small ads still seen in the backs of papers and magazines today.

Hair Cutter and Trimmer

In the 1950s, there was a fashion for cutting one's own hair at home. This gadget professed to be more than just a hair trimmer and that it replaced the hairdresser, the salon, and the barber, all in one go! The copy claims you can cut, trim, thin, shape, and style, that it saves you time and money, and that you can do it yourself exactly as you like it! But did it work? Or was it all too good to be true?

Get a Grip!

Hand Carpet Layer

Carpet laying is one area of work where tools are still very familiar today, but here are some early versions of today's grippers. This hand gripper is not that different at all.

Rope/String Tightener

Using Archimedes' screw principle, a pull on the handle twists the strands of rope or string and pulls them taut.

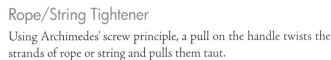

Mechanical Carpet Layer

The spikes go into the carpet and the lever on the side automatically tightens the material and ensures a good fit to the lounge floor.

If the Knife Slips . . .

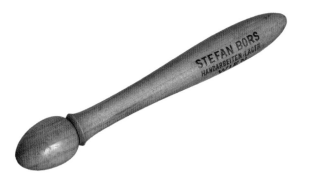

Pocket Heater

A simple, small '20s pocket warmer. Just the job for a stonking cold day in winter.

Finger Glove Darner

It wasn't just socks that needed darning in the Victorian era. If the fingertip of a glove had worn through it had to be mended—less of a throw-away society then. This finger darner did the job.

Butchers' Gloves

These metal chain gloves were worn by French butchers back in Edwardian times—a similar type of glove is still in use. Just like the chain mail of medieval times, the metal helped prevent cuts from slashing blades.

Tyres and Nails

Early tyres with inner tubes were particularly prone to punctures by nails, tacks, and screws, especially when cars were infrequent and not all roads were macadamised.

Automatic Nail Hammer

Eighty years ago this machine would automatically hammer nails into wood that needed joining. The hopper at the top fed the nails forward and the highly sprung mechanism bashed the nail into place. A serious bit of kit for the joiner of the day.

Tire Repairer and Vulcanizer

This machine held the rubber of the innertube in place while the glue adhered to the patch.

Now Then, Dobbin, Take Your Medicine

Horse Mouth Opener

It does seem a rather clunky device to ensure horse medicine can be given easily (also see p 275). It fits into the jaw of the animal and mechanically opens the mouth and holds it in position. It was used in the late 1800s.

Horse Measure

How many hands? A simple printed and sprung tape with its own attractive box. A must for the serious horse breeder.

Horse Tail Curler

Poultry Pecking Pickers

Pikgards

Sometimes you come across an invention that is out of one's own particular experience. I had never considered the possibility that chicken farmers might go to all the trouble of placing a metal guard on the beak of every single hen in a large free-range system to prevent pecking of fellow hens. We laugh about some husbands being hen-pecked, but this can be a serious problem amongst poultry, leading to disease and even death. The alternative to these metal beak guards was often beak trimming, but this practice is now outlawed. Plastic beak guards can still be bought along the same lines as these metal ones. Otherwise it is a case of managing the poultry well and making sure they have as stress free a life as possible. Of course, that might apply just as well to the hen-pecked household!

The Food We Eat

Foie Gras Stuffer

We apologise for listing this terrible little machine, but this system of fattening ducks and geese operates to this day.

To produce *foie gras* (the French term means "fatty liver"), workers ram pipes down the throats of male ducks twice each day, pumping up to two pounds of grain and fat into their stomachs—with geese three times a day and up to four pounds daily—in a process known as "gavage." The force feeding causes the birds' livers to swell to up to ten times their normal size. This example is late Victorian.

Meat Carcass Marker

This heavy brass roller has letters and numbers which, when inked and run along a carcass, provide a mark to establish the source of the meat. From the 1920s.

Knot a Problem!

Automatic Knotter

At work in the factory or the warehouse, this ingenious device could knot string or twine with just a quick press of the levers. Worn on the wrist, it must have made the job of the packer or dispatcher a great deal easier and would have been a boon to the mail order business.

A Yarn of Winding, Testing, and Weighing

Yarn Winder and Tester

Ensuring the thickness of the yarn in every order was an important part of quality control for any mill. This beautifully delicate antique brass yarn tester was made by Goodbrand & Co. in Manchester, England, around the 1920s. The base appears to be solid mahogany. The yarn to be tested was wound onto the winder and the bell rang when the yarn on the winder reached the length desired. The weight per length was then tested against a standard to judge the quality.

Thread Balance

Another beautifully crafted artefact of the textile industry is this balance scale for measuring very precisely the weights of standard lengths of cotton, worsted, or linen thread. It comes with three brass weights (one for each of the textiles) and still has its original case. The scale measures two and a half inches high. Precision engineering was never enough on its own—the objects also had to have aesthetic beauty.

Having a Happy Christmas

Make Your Own Cracker

The Victorians had little kits with all the components so that children could have some fun putting together crackers for each other—not a bad idea.

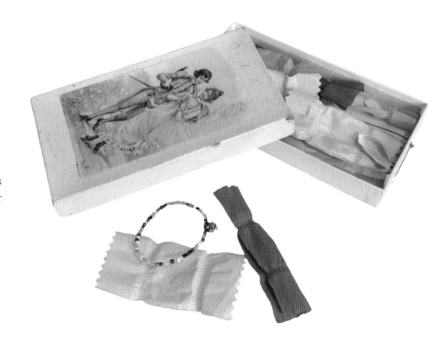

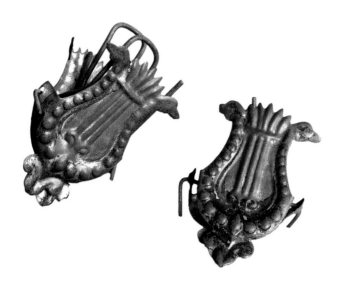

Candle Tree Clips

What happened before strings of electrical Christmas lights for the tree? The Victorians had these simple clips that held candles on the branches. The atmosphere created must have been really great—but the fire risk!

Decoration Lights

This nicely designed box from the late 1930s for Christmas decoration lights captures the atmosphere of the festival. The rather limited range of colours may seem a little odd to modern tastes.

Reaching the Parts Other Gadgets Cannot Reach

Balloon Cleaner

Victorian oil lamp glass shades soon became thick with soot and grime. This beautifully simple device allowed a cloth to be wrapped around it, inserted in the bulbous shade, expanded, and rotated to clean the inside of the glass. Really useful!

Bit Remover

Originally designed for the wine drinker, this "bit grip" was designed to remove bits of cork from wine bottles. Handy for all sorts of other nooks and crannies.

Jar Remover

Need to remove a jar from boiling water? Here is just the thing. An ideal tool for the kitchen. A use could be found for this today.

Pouring and Drenching

Bottle with Drinking Cup

A clever marketing ploy to sell the liquid with its own drinking vessel integrated in the base. No more swigging from the bottle!

Bottle with Wooden Cork

A very early stopper for aerated drinks. In Victorian times, many patents were taken out to stop the fizz going out of lemonade or sparkling water. This was a very rudimentary attempt to do the job.

Animal Drench

The plaque on the bottle explains its use and gives three rules when using — today, quite rightly, it would be many more, as farmers who have accidentally drenched themselves will testify.

Home Cures

Inhalation therapy has been used for over 2,000 years, but it was from the early nineteenth century that different types of inhalers were developed. In 1865, Dr. Nelson invented the improved Nelson inhaler. It is still manufactured today with very few modifications.

Steam Inhalers

As it says on the sides, steam inhalers are used to relieve spasmodic breathing, to disinfect bronchial secretions, and to facilitate expectoration of mucus.

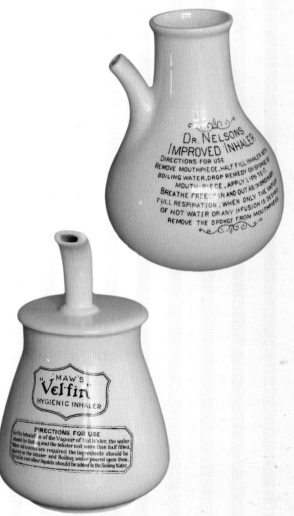

Holloway's Ointment

These amazing little pots, illustrated with an image of Hygeia, the goddess of health, and Hygeia's baby brother Telesphorus, were produced throughout the Victorian era. What it claimed to cure can be seen clearly on the pots.

Pill Making Machine

Dating from the nineteenth century, this very neat pill maker would have been used in pharmacies to make their own concoction of pain relieving medication. The chemist would roll the paste into a string and place it on the brass lower plate. Then he would push the top plate across, turning the strings of paste into small tablet-shaped balls. Once dry, the pills could be sold loose or packaged in tins—no doubt with labels extolling their efficaciousness!

Ironing the Clothes Whilst Having a Cuppa

This combination gadget is really so very cleverly designed that one feels it must have been specially commissioned, but by whom?

The flat iron base of the iron is heated electrically. It can then be used for its obvious purpose of ironing clothes or, by inverting, you can use it to boil water in the canister, ready to brew up a nice cup of tea.

The mystery is where and why would this be used? It wasn't used for camping—from where would the electricity be sourced? Perhaps it had an army use, mayhap in the billets or the barracks, allowing the soldiers to have a cuppa whilst getting the creases out of their uniforms.

Combination Iron and Kettle

Notice the handles for pouring the boiling water. All the pieces then tuck away perfectly, making a neat, portable unit with handles on the outside for ease of carrying.

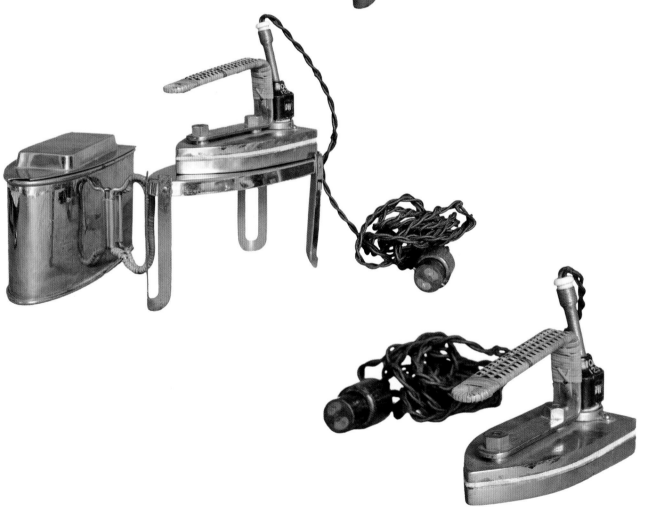

REALLY WEIRD BUT WONDERFUL

Gadgets can be serious and curious. They may be religious or morally improving. Some, sadly, are unpleasant, racist, or crude. Here is a miscellany of the good, bad, the rather beautiful, and the ugly.

This last section is a miscellany of the best and worst inventions from 150 years. There are items that are delightful and others that are a little depressing. There are gadgets that are downright dangerous and others whose real purpose is still in doubt—perhaps you can help?

There seems no area of life to which inventors would not turn their minds. Not everything worked and not everything was worth the effort of producing, but one has to marvel at the creativity they showed.

New gadgets, gizmos, and contraptions are still being produced today. No doubt many of these may one day find their way into a collection similar to this and no doubt, there will have to be a section for items to be wondered at, whether for their sheer awfulness or for their great beauty and ingenuity.

Cheep, Cheep! Look, No Drips!

Drip Collector

Late Victorian in manufacture, this lovely cast metal bird with its absorbent pad, attached by an elasticated band, soaked up those aggravating drips that always seem to emanate from the spouts of teapots.

This is just one example of the myriad of patents to do this one simple job. It's a shame that motorway cafés don't adopt a similar patent. Don't know about you, but I've never managed to pour a pot of tea without dripping. Or, better still, what about a foolproof non-drip spout design? Now that really would have the little birdie sing with joy!

You Liar—the Button Boy!

When out looking for items for the collection you come across some amazing stories linked to the artefact, even for the most everyday item.

Here is a case in point: a two-inch cast metal button with the words "YOU LIAR" emblazoned across the front. With it came the following story, which I believe has some truth in it.

In the days of tall ships, sails, and rigging, the "button" was the top part of the mast. In the Royal Navy, when young cadets had finished their training, the one who came out on top of his year became the "button boy," which gave them kudos, or some may think the dubious delight, to stand on that topmost part of the mast—on the "button."

Many were the cadets who spent an entire naval career bragging how they had been the button boy of their cohort, knowing full well that only their fellow cadets would know who had been atop the mast. The advent of photography changed all that. Now on passing out days, pictures were taken of the cadets decked across the cross beams of the ship, in the rigging, and on the "button."

The story goes that if a cadet should be discovered boasting in a pub in port how they had been the "button boy," their fellows would produce the photograph to disprove it and sew this button to the bragger's clothing, "YOU LIAR!"

A tall story for a tall ship? Or can anyone verify this nautical tale?

Thieves Beware!
The Ultimate Pocket Watch Protector

Watch Security

Placed with the chain on either side of the device nearest the watch, when a footpad attempted to steal the Victorian gentleman's watch three steel barbs leapt out to wound the thief, thus releasing the timepiece from his grasp and no doubt drawing blood, curses, foul language, and, if one was not careful, precipitating the miscreant into an act of violence against the person far worse than the original attempted offence. Jolly handy in a crowd for seeing off the villain. Not to be used today: you might be arrested for carrying an offensive weapon of your own!

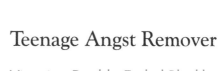

Teenage Angst Remover

Victorian Double-Ended Blackhead Remover

This simple and very small (only two inches) handy pocket gadget could be whipped out at the first sight of an ugly black pimple-like growth on the face.

Each end deals with a different sized blackhead. One press on the offending circle and out it would pop.

1930s Remover

Forty years on and manufacturers looked to produce something more modern and mechanical to do the same job. Though actually less effective than its Victorian predecessor, the Vacutex syringe and its like became the standard weapons of choice to reduce the anxiety of all blackhead sufferers.

Can Chew Gum and Fly!

Chewing Gum Necklace

This unbelievable 1898 novelty give-a-way by the manufacturers of gum seems a most amazing survivor. Who would believe that chewing gum was that old? The idea was that when the child was told to stop chewing—in school or by a harassed parent—they would take the offending material from their mouth, stick it on the spike, and close the lid. Then, when the coast was clear, they would whip out the gum again. Beats sticking it under the school desk, I guess.

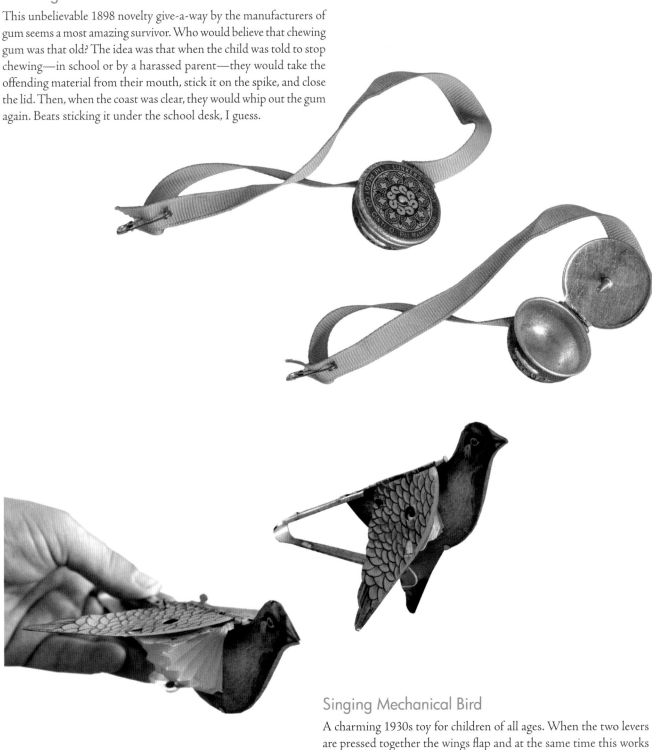

Singing Mechanical Bird

A charming 1930s toy for children of all ages. When the two levers are pressed together the wings flap and at the same time this works the paper bellows located below the wing to whistle a bird's song. Delightful and simple.

Having a Laugh

Chocolate Ants and Southend Air

There are two ways of looking at these daft gifts from the 1950s: either they are a cheerful way to bring a smile to the face or a terrible waste of money, or, of course, both. Can you imagine opening the tin of Southend air? Now what smell might greet you: cockles and mussels, or maybe just a whiff of burger and chips? Made in Harlesden, not Southend!

As for the chocolate ants, having never opened the tin we have no idea whether it contains coated ants in chocolat, just chocolate shaped as ants, or nothing at all—perhaps one day we will open it, though that would rather spoil the fun of guessing!

Just Slightly Near the Mark

Bust Improvers

Used to enhance the natural form in the 1950s, but similar fairly rudimentary devices were in use as breast prostheses following mastectomy back then.

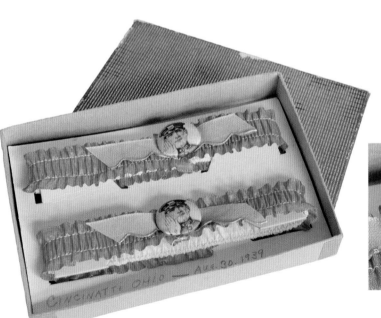

"Go No Further Garters"

Probably used as a novelty gift for those that were "tying the knot" in 1939, just for a laugh. Obviously American—the policeman is wearing the typical American uniform of the day. Definitely nudge, nudge, wink, wink.

Horrible Histories

Although I try not to collect any item that gives offence, it is sometimes a reflection on our past, when items appear that show some of our inhumanities and disregard for nature. These pictures are a stark reminder of what has gone before and what, in some parts of the world, may still be happening today.

Wild Bird Trap

A songbird would be placed in the cage. At the top of the device is a trap door. When the potential mate alighted on it, the door would swing open and the bird would be entrapped in the cage. Victorians were especially fond of "wild" songbirds and attractive finches in cages in the home. The goldfinch, for example, was nearly wiped out in Britain and numbers have only recovered relatively recently.

Cruel Dog Training Collar

This was used in training by brutal owners.

Body Manacles

It is unclear where this contraption was used—probably in a Victorian prison or mental institution. The two handcuffs were for the arms and the third, on the belt, would have been to control the wearer, manacling the arms to the side.

Racist Cap Gun

There is no hiding the nasty racist intent of this gadget aimed at children. The wording on the stock of the gun is explicit. This is social history told through a gadget at its most brutal.

How did it come to this level of hatred? After the American Civil War, railroads crossing the continent were pushed forward in haste. Initially, the main labour came from thousands of Irish immigrants, but more navvies were needed and so, in 1866, Union Pacific hired 3,000 Chinese. Their rival, Central Pacific, also took on Chinese workers. Soon 75% of their workforce was Chinese.

There was great animosity between the two factions. The Chinese were accused of being work-shy. Even their green tea was ridiculed, though by drinking boiled water the Chinese did not fall prey to dysentery, which struck down many of the Irish. In addition, Chinese pay was docked for their board while the Irish navvies' was not. Wanting equality, the Chinese went on strike in 1867 and demanded better wages and an end to whippings. Their food supplies were blocked and they were forced back to work.

Cap Gun

How very sad that the rivalry and bitterness between two races led to children being dragged into the dispute in this way. Sad, too, that this hatred of entire peoples is still with us today in so many parts of the world.

Not just the wording but the mechanism are blatantly racist. The cap is placed in the mouth. The leg is pulled back, the trigger is pulled, and the leg jumps up to give the Chinese man a kick in the posterior that closes the mouth, detonating the cap.

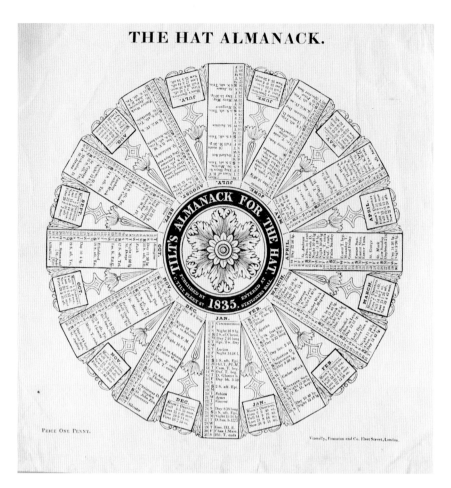

Keep It under Your Hat

An "Almanack" was a single sheet publication giving a whole year's calendar, along with details of astronomical data and general information.

This lovely example just predates Victoria's reign. One can imagine farmers at a market pulling it from inside their hat to check rent days.

These almanacks were often given away as a form of advertising, but Tilt's for 1835 was sold, costing one penny.

Pursing One's Stockings

Novelty Purse

Unbelievable, unusable, and, frankly, bizarre, but all the more interesting for that, this must be the most unlikely of all novelty gifts. From the 1930s, and surely not a commercial success. An "anything to make them laugh" product.

"Socking It Away"

The hose is no less than thirty-six inches long! No wonder the purse in its neck was a place to "sock it away!"

310

Dozen Thimbles

A daintier product. A lovely 1930s box containing twelve thimbles. Possibly used as a display in a haberdashery shop.

Cooling the Ardour

Sex Indicator

A very interesting product that could easily be misconstrued. By dangling the cotton-loaded weight over a mum to be you could predict the gender of the baby (or at least old wives can!): if it swings in a circular motion it's a girl; side to side like a pendulum, it's a boy. The claim is that it works at least 50% of the time!

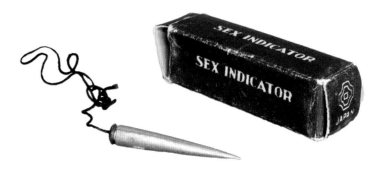

Aerosol Deodorant

In the 1950s, aerosol cans were beginning to be used in quantity. Notice the simple and unsophisticated design of the can, the crude and rudimentary button and nozzle, and the naïve artwork and logo—nothing like today's hard sell to keep you fresh.

The Fouler the Air . . .

Air Tester

We cannot think of a more gruesome looking practical product. It claims to give you an analysis of the vapour you are breathing.

It appears only to measure humidity in some way, but on the basis of that alone it claims to be able to advise on the best working conditions in factories to extract the most effort per worker.

Clockwork Air Freshener

As with today's ubiquitous air fresheners, if you can't actually get rid of the smell you can at least overpower it with scent. Just wind it up and the clockwork fan will spread a sweet or sickly aroma throughout the room.

A Transparent World

Glass Bird Feeders

The Victorians had a curious fascination with keeping small birds. Before plastics, glass was one of the principal media for small gadgets of all types.

Here are two examples of glass bird feeders. These were inexpensive items, but the catalogues of the time have an array of luxury glass bird accessories from which the discerning Victorian lady or gent could choose.

Glass Sweet Containers

Edwardian novelties, these containers—one a soldier and one a gun—were used to sell sweets to children, or at least to their poor pestered parents!

Sock Measure

Supporting the troops in WWI. The wife, mother, or sweetheart would send out the tape, keep the knitting instructions and hope against hope that the next letter back was a series of measurements and not the dreaded "If you get this letter, I just want you to know . . ."

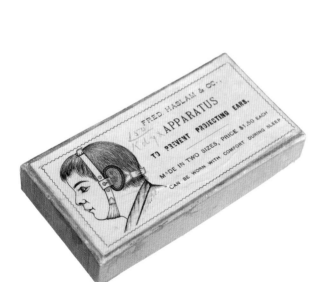

Ear Flattener

With the greatest respect, we wonder whether, had Prince Charles been aware of this Edwardian product, it might have changed his whole persona.

Notice also that the "apparatus" was supplied in two sizes: could they have been "sticky-out" and "jumbo?"

Wrinkle Eradicator

Another example of "nothing new under the sun." Notice also the unusual choice of brand name. Was it really only used by "Two Women" or by many thousands? And why? Well, the reason is obvious: as the two ladies might have said, "Because we're worth it."

"Watch the Birdie!"

Bird Caller

There are several of these in the collection, and each one made a different call to lure unsuspecting birds. This one uses a rubber concertina: just press. Poor little birdies!

Bird Roaster

Once caught, this was their fate. This French device skewered the bird. It was then pushed between the bars of an open fire. It could even be revolved on the skewers. Done to a turn, as you might say.

Photographers Tweeting Bird

Here it is, the source of the phrase "watch the birdie." Especially in the days of long-exposure film, the photographer had to find a way to keep children's attention, or even recalcitrant adults! Attached to the hole in the middle of the up strut was a rubber tube. There was water in the bottom. With one hand on the shutter of the camera the photographer blew into the tube. The pipe trilled and the air forced the bill of the bird to move, so it appeared to be chirping. Who's a clever boy, then?

Pistol and Pocketknife

We believe this to be a slightly earlier version of the pistol displayed in the advertisement as it was still unpatented, possibly from the early 1920s.

The Defender

This simple, lethal contraption is somewhat disturbing on a number of levels. It brings self-defence to the camp fire. It is easy to operate: simply place a bullet in the chamber; pull the lever outward, turning it into a trigger; give it a hard pull, and the weapon fires its shot, with potentially deadly consequences.

Takes Your Breath Away

Some things are always with us—or at least with some of us, anyway—and one perennial problem is bad breath. Will a cure-all never be found? In Victorian times as now, if it cannot be cured, at least it may be disguised.

Made of tin, this small pocket device allowed those wishing to have a fresh smelling mouth to "sweeten the breath and refresh the mouth."

It works by turning one-half of the container till the hole appears, allowing a cachou to appear.

Prince Albert died in 1861. It does seem strange this dispenser of breath fresheners would have been the vogue well after the prince passed away. It may also seem strange that such a product should have been so clearly associated with Prince Albert's name—surely the prince consort did not suffer from bad breath? Whatever would Victoria have said?

Six-in-One Novelty Promotion

This give-away takes multi-functionalism to new heights. It breaks down to six uses: dice, put and take, pen, pencil, cigarette holder, and compass.

Pull-Apart Pen

Probably from the 1950s, it was a give-away from a company, the name of which only appears on the original box, so who thought up this idea has lost some of the promotional punch from its distribution. It is an amazing novelty. My one concern, and perhaps suggesting an earlier date, is the racist word in the ditty that accompanies the pen.

Beautiful and Baffling

A very bizarre artefact: a key that opens into a fan. So far, we can find no reason for such an unusual Victorian item. The very best we can come up with is that it was part of a magician's armoury of tricks, but even that feels a bit far-fetched—does a reader have an idea?

The Sanitary Artist!

Promotional Water Colour Palette

To discover the use of this rather clinical looking but exceptionally well made product from the famous toilet and sink manufacturer Armitage took some working out. We believe it is a water-colourist's palette, with a place for paints, water, and a mixing bowl, but why would a sink manufacturer sell or give away these ceramic mixers?

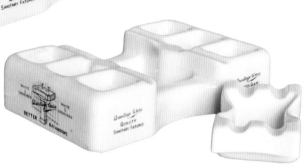

Words from the Bible

Turning Biblical Words

This object is something of a mystery. You turn each of the seven wheels in turn to create a sentence, but nine times out of ten the words are just a jumble. Were you supposed to dwell on each word in turn? Or was it particularly propitious if you happened on a properly formed biblical saying?

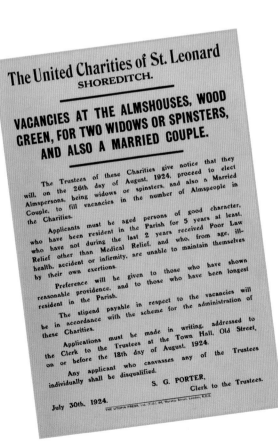

Religion and Charity

Charity Public Notice

An interesting notice offering places in the almshouses for those in need—the words speak for themselves.

Religious Tracts

Why were tracts from the Bible presented in this form? Were they used in church or perhaps Sunday School? I have been told you would find them on shop counters in Victorian times, allowing customers to pick one out at random to give them spiritual comfort for the day.

Dainty Names

Name Wafers

A lovingly preserved complete box set of named stickers that would have been on show in a stationery retailer in Edwardian times. It covers a range of the most popular feminine names of the period, such as Cissie, Lottie, Lizzie, Queenie, Edith, and Nellie.

Each packet contains twenty-five wafers (the name of the product at that time) and are gummed on the rear to allow them to be stuck onto notepaper, envelopes, or even postcards, personalising the message.

It claimed to be "the most inexpensive stationery decoration ever issued."

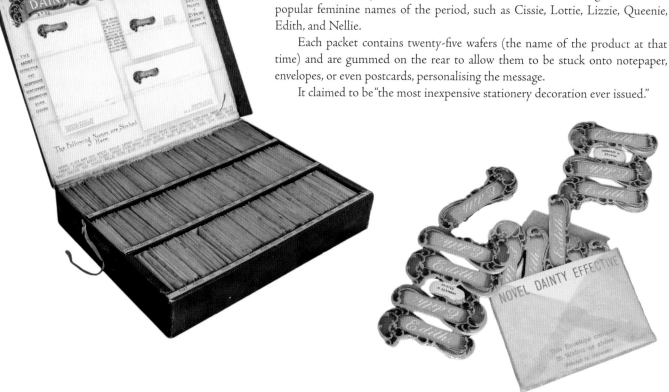

Queen Victoria's Family

Name: Queen Victoria
Full Name: Alexandrina Victoria
Born: May 24, 1819, at Kensington Palace
Parents: Edward, Duke of Kent (son of George III) and Victoria of Saxe-Coburg-Saalfeld
Relation to Elizabeth II: Great-great-grandmother
Ascended to the throne: June 20, 1837, at eighteen years
Crowned: June 28, 1838, at Westminster Abbey
Married: Albert, son of Duke of Saxe-Coburg-Gotha
Children: Four sons, including the future Edward VII, and five daughters
Died: January 22, 1901, at Osborne, Isle of Wight, eighty-one years old
Buried at: Frogmore
Succeeded by: Her son, Edward VII.

Jubilee Souvenir Plate

Made of papier-mâché, this plate holds a mystery: why would Raphel Tuck, a publisher of postcards, produce an item so out of their normal range of manufacture? Possibly as a give-away to their buyers? Or perhaps it was a product to sell to the public for the Jubilee of 1887.

On the rear of the plate is printed the key to all those on the front, who they are in the family, and their ranking —an amazing and beautiful relic to have lasted in this condition for 130 years.